The Biggest Financial Mistakes Retirees Make!

Dennis J. O'Keefe, CFP

Table of Contents

Preface

As I prepared to update this manuscript in 2016, I had a new client ask me if I wrote the book to scare people.

That gave me some pause. Did I? Had I set out to put fear in the hearts of thousands of people between the ages of 50 and 65?

That has never been my intention. The world is more complicated than it was in 1975. The financial world is exponentially more complicated than it was in 1975. Keeping up with all of the nuances and rules is hard.

Just take IRA withdrawal rules as an example. You can begin no-penalty withdrawals the year you turn 59½. How many people think they have to be exactly 59½ to take that withdrawal? And how many people think that after 59 ½, there is no taxes due? (Both are wrong.)

The year you reach 70½, you must take *minimum* distributions from your IRA. If you thought the rules at 59½ were complicated, think of how much more so they become when you are 11 years older.

That is just one small aspect of your planning. And the mistakes are costly. Taxes can reach 50% or more.

Think on that: Mistakes could cost you 50% or more. Not fraud. A simple mistake.

Mistakes can cost you thousands in taxes. They can cost you years of income from bad investments. They can leave you vulnerable to a lawsuit. They can waste a third of your estate in needless taxes and fees.

Let's say you had a house on the side of one of the Hollywood hills. One day a structural engineer tells you that the footings on your house are bad and if there is a minor earthquake, your home is going to go tumbling into the valley.

Did he scare you? Yes, I guess he did. Did it change your situation or did it better clarify; allowing you to make the decisions to correct your previous oversight? Absolutely!

If this book scares you, I'm sorry. But if it motivates you to properly prepare for these circumstances, then I have done my job.

I've spent considerable time updating and clarifying many portions of this book. It has been 10 years since the first publishing and we've seen significant political changes, Universal Health Care and major changes to the Tax and Estate laws (as well as major changes to the Probate laws in Massachusetts.)

My hope is that this edition will be timely for another 8-10 years.

Please enjoy the book. I hope it sheds some light on your current financial situation and ensures your retirement success as well.

June, 2016

Congratulations, Retiree!
You've Done It! Now What?

Do you remember your first day of school? Do you remember that feeling of excitement and apprehension? It may have been kindergarten. Or high school. Or even college. You couldn't wait until you got there, but there was also a certain apprehension. Life was changing, and you knew it couldn't go back to the way it was. Irrevocably, things had changed. You were flying without a net.

For most, retirement is the exact same way. You've lived a certain way for thirty years or more. And now you must face a new way of life. Even though the old way of life was great. No more getting up at o'dark thirty. Or waiting all year for those 3 or 4 weeks of vacation.

No more. Now you can get up when you want, go on vacation 365 days a year and wear pajamas and fuzzy slippers until 11 o'clock (or later) if you want.

Except you won't have a safety net anymore. There is no more job to fall back on. No one is going to send you a paycheck every week. You are your own paycheck. Sure you've worked hard and you are pretty sure you can make it, but if you're wrong, how can you go back?

There are no second chances here. You can't decide at 70 or 75 that you want a do-over and go back to your old job. The decisions you make today impact the rest of your life – and the life of your spouse and others who depend on you. I don't blame you for worrying.

Several years ago, I counseled a close friend who was retiring. Between his property and investments, his portfolio ran into the millions. Based on his modest spending, he would never want for money. We were going over his retirement projections and I was explaining to him what his yearly spending budget would look like.

"But where does it come from?" he asked apprehensively.

"Well, some of the money will come from Social Security when you turn 62." I explained. "Some will come from your pension starting at age 65. And the rest will come from your portfolio before and after that time."

He grabbed my arm and with a look of panic, blurted, "But where will I get money to buy groceries *NEXT WEEK?*"

I have always been able to sympathize with the stresses of retiring. But that one meeting really hit home to me. That's when I saw what keeps people awake at night in the days, weeks, and months both before, and shortly after, retirement.

If you are considering retiring within the next few years, I'm sure all of these thoughts have crossed your mind.

- **How will I get the income I need in retirement?** Where will that cash come from? How will I pay the bills? Will Social Security be solvent in twenty years or will I have to find another source of income?

- **What tax minefields are waiting for me?** What is the best way to take a 401(k) distribution? Can I still make an IRA contribution? Will I owe more to Uncle Sam on April 15th than I have in available cash?

- **What happens if I get sick?** Who will take care of me? Is my spouse capable of caring for me? What if I need specialized care?

- **How am I going to keep track of all my investments?** How do I know which ones are having trouble? Should I follow CNBC or *Money Magazine?* What happens if we have another crash like in 2008?

My goal in this book is to help answer some of these questions. I also want to show you some other questions you may never have thought to ask.

I don't want to scare you, but most of us only have one shot to retire. Making mistakes is not an option many of us can afford. I will give you as much of my 25 years of my retirement planning experience as I can. But this book is *by no means a comprehensive treatise on the subject of retirement.*

The rules alone for the tax issues you could face would fill a room with books. Investment advice could fill another. Estate planning a third.

Use this book to spark ideas, not solve all of your financial issues relating to retirement. Don't look at the examples as cookie-cutter situations that you can copy and paste into your financial life.

Your retirement will be vastly different than anyone else you know. You and your next-door neighbor could work the same job, make the same pay and have the same number of children yet have VASTLY different retirement strategies.

There are few, if any, rules of thumb here. And the few that there are have gaping exceptions to them. To go back to our *first day of school* idea, think back to your old spelling rules – and all of their exceptions. "I" before "E". . . except after "C". . . except for. . . For every rule of thumb in finance, I can name you a person I've encountered that turned that rule on its head.

This book is laid out around the seven biggest retirement mistakes I've seen people make. These are common pitfalls that can ruin you financially – sometimes without you realizing it.

Some of the mistakes retirees make is like heart disease or a slow-moving cancer. It doesn't become known until years from now – when it is too late to correct the error. "If only we had done something sooner. . . but we never knew!"

There are certainly other mistakes people make in their retirement planning. These are the "doozies" as my dad would say. The ones that more people get wrong and that every retiree should get right.

Each chapter will walk you through one basic mistake. By the end, you will have a clear picture of the areas you are deficient and at least a direction as to how to correct them.

As I mentioned, I have been counseling people on retirement issues for 25 years. It's all that I do. I specialize in helping people retire. The rules are complex. The situations are always different. I won't say I've seen it all, because each time I think I have, I see something new. But I've seen a lot. I hope that through this book, I can show you some of what I've seen.

Failing To Plan!

Unless you live under a rock, you've heard of Tiger Woods. While he's had his medical and marital difficulties in the last several years, we all can agree that Tiger has changed the game of golf forever. And it all started with one simple tournament in 1997 called the Masters Tournament.

The Masters is very appropriately titled. It is arguably the toughest tournament in the pro-golf series. The fairways are narrow. The putting greens are like glass. And the sand traps are deep.

In any given year, there are several golfers vying for the prize at the Masters. Throughout the four-day tournament, most of the daily scores are very close – and very high. (Remember, golf is a game of the *lowest* score, not the highest.) The course is that tough. But in 1997, something unheard of happened.

Tiger Woods succeeded in winning the tournament shortly after it began. He took a commanding lead on Thursday and continued to build to an unheard of 12 stroke lead when he was done on Sunday. He scored 18 under par for the 4 days. The next closest golfer scored only a 6 under par. It was amazing.

Now if you are unfamiliar with golf, I'll tell you a little secret. In every golf tournament, putting is what separates the champion from the other players. It is so difficult to get that little ball into that little hole that an otherwise perfect game can be ruined less than 30 feet from the hole. And as I mentioned earlier, in the Masters Tournament, the greens are like glass. They make them extra hard to separate the men from the boys. And Tiger outputted every single golfer out there that weekend.

But I know that I can get any able-bodied American to beat Tiger Woods at putting in about 15 minutes. I just have to give you a quick lesson. . .

and then blindfold Mr. Woods. Then spin him around so he doesn't know where the hole is. Then you can beat him every day of the week.

"But he can't see the hole!" you say.

"How can he play if he doesn't know where he's going?!"

Exactly! And how do you expect to retire successfully if you don't even know where you are going? Are you in the neighborhood? Are you even in the right part of town?

18

Planning is the single, most effective technique to have a safe and secure retirement!

It worked a hundred years ago, it worked fifty years ago, and it works today!

See, the reason most of us aren't going to win the retirement game, is that we don't follow this crucial sequence when it comes to managing our finances (or playing golf for that matter):

✓ Figure out where you are right now.
✓ Figure out where you want to be.
✓ Get a true understanding of the options you have available to you.
✓ Develop a plan that will provide the right "course" to follow.
✓ Make the changes necessary to get the plan going.
✓ Watch your progress, and make the proper adjustments to keep the plan "on course".

Makes a lot of sense, doesn't it?

It's the same process you go through every day whether planning a trip to the mall or planning your vacation.

Could you imagine how you could get through your daily life without following this sequence of events?

Let's say you have a golf date tomorrow. Could you imagine how chaotic your life would be if you didn't know the weather forecast for tomorrow? And you didn't know when your tee-time was? And you didn't know where your clubs were, nor did you know who you were playing with? *Worst of all, didn't even know where you were playing?*

I know that sounds silly because in our day to day activities we always know all those things! For simple repetitive tasks, we do this as a matter of course.

But at one point in your life, you didn't do it that way, did you? You had all of your gear – for a trip to the links or a trip to the mall – ready the night before. You called and confirmed with everyone who was in your party. You consulted a map so you knew where you were going.

But you don't do that anymore, do you? You have this whole golf or shopping thing down pat.

How many times have you done this "retirement" thing? First time, right? So that means we need to get back to the basics of planning.

Success Begins with a Plan!

Do you truly know where you are today? Are you certain you have specific goals of where you want to be financially? Can you say that you know all the choices you have available to you? Have you set up a plan to get where you want to be? **Or, like most people, are you winging it as you go along???**

In all the years I've been helping people win the game of money, I have found one common theme.

It is not their age, or occupation, or sex, or income, or any of those things that make a winner. The one common attribute is that *they make a constant effort to plan for their future.*

That's it.

It may not sound very glamorous or romantic. But it's simple, and it works.

Isn't that always the way? The most effective things in life are the most simple and basic.

Your retirement will constantly be under attack by changes in the economy, changes in government, and changes in your own life situation. You need to plan for your own future now more than ever!

Make sense? I hope so. Because this topic is very important to me, and to you. It's important to me because helping people successfully plan is my livelihood. It's important to you because planning is the best weapon you'll have to make sure you live the way you want during retirement!

I've been counseling families on retirement planning since 1991. In that time, I've seen some fantastic successes and some spectacular failures. While I help my clients on a wide range of financial issues ranging from investments to insurance to estate planning to income taxes, it's the planning that is the most important.

A poor plan, or no plan, will ensure you never succeed in retirement. I can't tell you how sad it makes me when someone makes all of their retirement decisions by the seat of their pants.

REAL LIFE STORY: How Not To Plan For Retirement!

This is the first of many stories taken from my client files. Names and some details have been changed for privacy. But the basic facts are true. These stories will help emphasize the successes and failures you can encounter when planning for retirement.

Let me tell you a story of a client of mine. Jeff was fortunate. He had worked for over 25 years with his employer and discovered one day that he was eligible for early retirement – at age 49.

"Great!" He told me. "Now I can go do something I really love. Like teaching or something."

That "or something" had me worried. But there was no shaking Jeff. He was bound and determined to leave his employer.

"I'm not in a big rush," he told me. "I'll live off the severance for a year or so, then go back to work doing something. I'm marketable."

Granted, it was a sweet deal. He got a year's pay in severance. He also got a big boost to his pension – which was converted to a lump-sum cash buyout. Plus he had a fair amount in his 401(k) plan. Provided he got another job, he would be swimming in retirement capital.

A year later though, he still hadn't gone back to work. And he was burning through money fast. A job was a necessity at that point.

At our next meeting, he said, "You know. I've got no equity in my home here. I'm thinking of selling out and buying something down south where it's cheaper to live. I'd like it if I never saw snow again."

I asked how he was going to pay for a new home with no income and no ready-cash to fall back on.

"I've got it all figured out." Jeff said.
"I'm going to take my 401(k) plus my pension
buy-out and use that money to buy a piece of
property. That way I can live rent free."

And that's just what he did (against
my advice). He withdrew $500,000 from his
retirement plans to fund his short-term goals.
Did he buy a $500,000 house? No. He
bought a $260,000 house.

**Where Did The Rest Of The Money
Go?**

Taxes, of course. Jeff paid federal tax
on the distribution of up to 35%. Then state
taxes. Then a 10% early withdrawal penalty.
All told, he paid almost $240,000 in taxes, as
detailed here.

Federal taxes paid:	$165,000
Penalty for early withdrawal:	$50,000
State income tax:	$23,000

Jeff never had a plan for retirement.
He never planned further than a year in
advance. I don't know what happened to Jeff.
I hope that he figured out how to better plan
before he retires. . . again.

Average Retirement Means Living On Less!

Let's look at the average American and how well they plan for retirement.

According to the Social Security Administration, Social Security checks account for 38% of the income retirees receive. Yet the average yearly payout from Social Security is only about $15,500.[i]

Using some simple math, that means the average retiree lives on a little less than $41,000 per year. While thankfully that is above the poverty level, it isn't much compared to what the average retiree was earning during their working years.

Many sources say that the average retiree lives on somewhere between 70 and 80% of their working-year's income.

Are these retirees buying 20% less groceries? Are they going on 20% less vacations? Do they go out to eat 1-2 fewer times per week?

Or are they spending less because they have less income than before?

What's even worse is that according to the Bureau of Labor Statistics, almost a third of people over the age of 65 work – and possibly up to 20% of retirement income comes from wages!ⁱⁱ **Retirees are living on so little, they have to get jobs in order to make ends meet!**

It reminds me of a commercial several years ago. A *little old man* of about 70-75 gets dressed. He smiles and kisses his wife, takes his lunch, leaves the beautiful old, well maintained Victorian home on Main Street, USA and heads off to work. . .

AT McDONALD'S!

The very next scene he's turning around with a big smile on his face while taking a customer order. (I've never figured out why he brings his lunch to work. Maybe he knows something we don't about McDonald's food.)

Can you imagine retiring and jumping out of bed 5 days a week to work at McDonald's? I know I can't. My golden years will be spent doing what I want to do. And if it's working, it's because I *choose* to work. Not because I have to spend all day as the french-fry guy to make ends meet.

And of course, McDonald's isn't telling the whole story. How many people living on Main Street, USA in a 3-color-scheme Victorian with a full porch are working at McDonald's? The reality is that a retiree works at McDonald's because they don't have sufficient income from their pension, savings and Social Security. They'll never live on Main Street, USA because they can barely make ends meet.

So you can see how important it is to have a plan. And a good one. Whether you are a few years from retirement, or you just retired, a plan today will save you a lot of heartache later on.

Remember To Work The Plan!

The odds are good that you are either working at a large company or have worked at one in the past. And if your company was like most, you had a sea of binders on, over or under your desk.

Every two to three years – sometimes more often – the corporate bigwigs decided to roll out some new plan to either boost morale, save money, make money, or save made money while boosting morale.

Along with that plan came a binder. You know those plans.

Sadly, only a choice few of these plans were ever implemented. (Usually the ones that looked exciting or had some sort of financial incentive tied to them.) The rest only resulted in an unused binder and cost untold numbers of trees their lives,.

But just for the sake of example, what if just one of those unused plans would have actually made a difference in your company?

What if that one plan could have tripled the price of the company stock and doubled your salary?

We'll never know because it was never implemented. It sat dormant on everyone's shelves waiting for the next big thing to come along.

Years ago, I met with a couple who had a previous financial advisor of sorts. At our first meeting, they presented me with their previous financial plan. It was a padded leatherette binder with their names embossed across the cover in gold.

They were very proud of that plan. It was kept in a safe, but accessible place so they could look at it when needed.

And when I say "look at it as needed," I don't mean refer to it and evaluate their progress. No. I mean they looked at it and thought, "Well, there it is!" I probably read more pages in that plan than they ever did.

Even with the most perfect plan, if we don't take the steps to implement that plan, nothing will be accomplished. It's the same way with a financial plan. If none of the steps are carried out, <u>nothing</u> will be accomplished.

Some of those steps may not be exciting or glamorous. In fact, they might be downright boring. Things like having your will updated or increasing your automobile liability coverage may actually cost you time and money in the short run. But if any results are to be seen, these steps need to be taken.

In order to retire successfully, you are going to have to *do* some thing. *(Or get someone else to do it for you. But more on that later on.)* You are going to have to take actions. And those small, relatively pain-free steps today will reap huge dividends in retirement.

Retiring With Blinders On!

REAL LIFE STORY: Making Bad Bets With Your Retirement!

Many years ago, I was counseling Jack and Gail, a couple nearing retirement. They had done an excellent job planning. Their debt was minimal. They had put all three children through college. And both had worked hard at jobs with large stable companies with large stable pensions.

During my initial meetings with Jack and Gail, I was excited about their retirement prospects and praised their planning and foresight. Between their modest savings and reasonable pensions, they would be well off.

Later that year, Gail received what she had been waiting for – a retirement "package" from her employer. At 58, she could now reap the benefits of all her hard work.

Jack, almost 64, was planning on leaving his employer shortly thereafter. He didn't have to wait for a "package." He had enough years of service that it didn't matter.

So that November, Gail retired. Jack was supposed to retire at year-end, but decided that one more year would help. Financially, it wouldn't make much of a difference. Looking back, I think he was afraid to retire.

This didn't sit well with Gail. She wanted to travel. To appease her, Jack bought a small motor-home in April. He promised he'd only stay until June 30. Then he'd retire and they could see the country.

But you can see where this story is going. Jack didn't retire on June 30th. He forcibly retired in August when Gail was diagnosed with an aggressive form of cancer. He didn't retire to travel the country but to care for his ailing wife.

In December, Gail passed away. I was so sad for Jack. He had delayed his retirement for no other reason than a false sense of insecurity. But I only knew half of the story.

In early spring, I sat down with Jack to help him with the financial aspects of Gail's death. At that meeting, Jack dropped a bombshell on me.

"I don't know how I'm going to get along." He began. "I can't make ends meet without Gail's pension."

I was stunned. "Jack, you'll get half of her pension. That, plus your pension, will be more than enough to carry you."

Jack's eyes were downcast. With barely a whisper, he replied, "We didn't take a survivor option on Gail's pension."

He had decided while Gail was filling out her retirement paperwork that the odds were with him. He was a man. He was older. It was a good bet that Gail would out-live him. And if they chose a life-only pension for Gail, it would net them an extra $120 per month. The odds were just too good to pass up.

If he was in Las Vegas at a Blackjack table, this was a smart move. But in real life, his downside wasn't just the money he put down on that bet. The downside was his entire retirement.

We had run the numbers. The $120 per month wasn't vital to Jack and Gail maintaining their current standard of living. The $120 was nice, but it was icing on the cake. Jack bet Gail's entire pension for an extra four bucks a day. And he lost.

Ultimately, Jack's daughter and her family moved in with him. He couldn't make ends meet with only his pension and savings. All of his retirement dreams were shattered by a quick decision

Haste Makes Bad Decisions!

Why did Jack decide to take a $120 per month gamble? I don't really know. I'm sure the pressure of having to make a decision on Gail's retirement package in a short period of time had something to do with it.

I firmly believe that if Jack had more time to review his options – *especially with someone helping him to look at the big picture* – he'd have made the right decision.

Retiring is difficult. I won't kid you. It's a massive change of lifestyle. If you don't know the answers to all of the questions, you are liable to make bad choices. Especially with the clock ticking on your decision.

If you are still working, you might not be able to relate. But to those who've already retired, you know that gut-wrenching paralyzing fear that can make even the simplest decisions a nightmare.

I have had a multi-million-dollar client who was unable to decide whether or not to have a distribution check mailed to him or electronically deposited because the anxiety was so great.

Stress of retirement? Now you folks who haven't retired really think I'm off my rocker, right? There is no stress. This is retirement!

Think of it this way. Today, you go to work. Every payday, you get a check. Every single time. There is one (or two in a dual-income family) source of income. You work, you get paid, you pay the bills.

But what happens when you retire? Where does all of that money come from? Your pension? Social Security? We've already seen in the last chapter that those sources alone won't fund your retirement.

All of a sudden, you are spending down your retirement savings and investments. There is no more safety net. You can't go work for another 10 years to make it all back if you screw up. That job that you may have grown to dislike while waiting for that magical retirement date is a safety blanket. And one day you have it. The next, it's gone forever.

Pension Options: Which One To Take?

We've already seen with Jack and Gail that in most cases, a survivor option of some sort is important. That's pretty easy. Although in some cases – usually with municipal pensions – that survivor option may be too expensive.

There are alternatives. Many municipal retirees forgo the survivor benefits but purchase adequate life insurance to protect their spouse should they die early. How much insurance do you need? It really depends on your situation. I can tell you this: *You don't want some slick-looking insurance agent who's rubbing his palms together calculating his commission as he outlines the "proper coverage" for you.*

Another popular issue relating to pensions today is a **Lump Sum Buyout**. With this option, you get to receive a large check immediately instead of a monthly check the rest of your life.

Is it a good deal? It can be. Let's look at the pros and cons of a Lump Sump Buyout.

PRO: You get full control of your money, but
CON: You have to do all of your own investing.

PRO: You are protected against corporate insolvency, but
CON: There is no creditor protection.

PRO: You get to choose when and how much money you spend annually, but
CON: There is no protection from Medicaid/Long Term Care.

PRO: If you die early in retirement, your heirs receive the remainder of your lump sum, but
CON: You might screw up and lose all of your retirement assets within a few years.

There is no easy answer. For some people, a lump-sum offer is great. For others, it is a nightmare.

For instance, I had two clients who retired a few years ago. They both worked in the same department. One was an experienced investor with many other assets and investments. For him, a buyout was a natural fit.

His co-worker had minimal savings, had never invested, and was in a tighter situation, financially. For him, a pension afforded him the security of knowing that no matter what, he would receive a check each and every month. *For every individual, there will be a different answer!*

Finally, you must make sure the lump sum you are being offered is reasonable. In *most* cases, the company wants you to take the lump sum and will add financial incentive to do so. But I have also seen cases where the lump sum offer was too low. You **must** do the calculations to make sure you know which option is best for you. And as we've discussed already – these calculations should be done **before** you receive a retirement "package."

Monthly Pension Options!

In some cases, you don't have a choice of a lump-sum payment. Or you decide to take an annuity. But which option do you choose?

Not that long ago, you would be offered two options if you decided to take a monthly pension: Payments for your life, or payments for your life with a survivor's option for your spouse. Today, many folks have an option for a 10-year payout, selecting alternate beneficiaries, life-certain payments (which pay for at least 5 or 10 years, but will pay for life otherwise), and many others.

Basically, there are a lot of non-choices in there. I'll let you in on a little secret. All of those options are great, but for the vast majority of people, it will come down to two options: Life-only or some sort of spousal survivor's benefit. The people that benefit from the other options are few and far between in my experience.

Should You Take A Survivor Option?

This was basically Jack and Gail's question. Should they take a survivor option? And if not, what can you do to protect the spouse?

38

Most people I talk to who are going to receive a pension discuss with me the possibility of taking a life-only payout and purchasing life insurance to protect their spouse. This is a serious decision that cannot be taken lightly.

Let me stop for a moment and let that sink in. ***THIS IS A SERIOUS DECISION THAT CANNOT BE TAKEN LIGHTLY!*** Making a mistake in this can cause serious harm to your spouse. I cannot stress how important this decision is.

To add more stress, the people that will counsel you on this issue are biased. I don't want to say that every life insurance agent out there is a liar. That's not true. But you should know where the bias is for the agent running your calculation, right?

The calculations are complex enough that I've seen situations where the cost of a pension's survivor's option is low, yet an insurance agent is (incorrectly) arguing for a life-only pension and insurance. In those cases, either the insurance premium will eventually cost more than the cost of a survivor option *or* you haven't purchased nearly enough insurance to cover the risk.

You need to go over this calculation in detail with whomever you hire to run the figures for you. You need to know what they are assuming your spouse's life expectancy is. You need to know what sort of investment rate-of-return they plan for you. (Hint: If it's over 10%, heck, even if it's over 8%, run away. They are playing with fire and your retirement security is the kindling!)

You need to know what sort of guarantees the insurance policy has to ensure that your premium will **NOT** rise. And if someone tells you, "I'm a professional, you should just trust me," **DON'T!**

There are no absolutes in this game. But I can give you some guidelines, based on the cases I've worked on. For most of the corporate pensions I've looked into for clients, the cost for a survivor option is pretty cheap. It certainly was in Jack and Gail's case.

For most of the municipal pensions I've looked at, assuming the pensioner is healthy, it is usually better to take a life-only pension and purchase *ADEQUATE* insurance.

This is not a game. I can't stress that enough. You need to have the best people doing their best work on calculations such as lump-sum vs. pension and pension vs. life insurance. This is no time for you to do a favor for your nephew Ricky who needs a leg-up in the "financial services" field.

And this is probably not the time to be trying to figure this out yourself. If you don't have a financial background, you don't know all the ins and outs of these calculations. I have had many smart clients try to do these things themselves. And invariably, they left themselves wide open because they focused on what they thought was the major issue and ignored other issues that were of equal or greater importance.

401(k)'s and Other Retirement Plans – How To Get Money Prior To 59½!

I'm sure you know that if you withdraw money from your retirement accounts prior to age 59½, you will be taxed on the amount, plus pay a tax *penalty* of an additional 10%. But what if you want to retire at 55? Or 50? Virtually all of your money is locked up in retirement plans. Can you access that money early?

Yes, Virginia, you CAN retire prior to age 60 and gain access to your 401(k), 403(b), TSA, 457 and/or IRA. While these options are becoming more popular, only a handful of people realize that there are exceptions to the rules governing the 10% penalty tax.

The Three D's!

Probably the most common way people access retirement account monies prior to age 59½ is via the three D's.

1. Death
2. Disability
3. Divorce

Now obviously these aren't real exciting choices for the account owner. If you are dead, you really can't spend any of the money. If you are disabled, you can't truly enjoy your nest egg either. And finally, if you are getting divorced, it isn't **you** who will be spending that money – it's your former spouse.

In all three of these examples, someone (usually other than you) is exempted from the 10% penalty tax because of a *hardship.* I want to make you aware of these exceptions, but I hope that you don't need to use them.

Retirement After Age 55!

There is another exception to the 10% rule: If you retire *AFTER* age 55, your company sponsored accounts - namely your 401(k) – is exempted from the 10% tax.

Let me list a whole bunch of caveats to that rule. This is one of the most confusing rules I see people face.

1. If you retire at 54, you don't qualify.
2. Your IRA does not qualify.
3. Your old 401(k) with a former employer does not qualify.
4. Your spouse's plans do not qualify (unless he or she retires after age 55 as well.)
5. If you roll your 401(k) into an IRA, you forfeit this strategy.
6. If you retire at 54, you do not qualify! (It needs to be said twice. You need to turn 55 first THEN retire. No exceptions.)

So if you are retiring a *little* early, this can be a big advantage to you. But like anything else, you have to be super-careful. No one is watching out for you at the IRS or your employer or your 401(k) provider. This is all on you or you and your advisor. One slip and all of your planning is for naught.

The Ultimate Exception – 72t!

There is one final important exception to the 10% penalty tax. It is called a 72t or *Substantially Equivalent Periodic Payment* calculation. And if it sounds complicated, it's supposed to. Because it is.

What Uncle Sam says is that if you turn your retirement account into a self-directed pension, you will avoid any penalties. Sounds easy enough, right? Wrong! Here are just some of the rules you have to follow:

a. You must take out a substantially equal payment based on any of three different government calculations.

b. If you are married, you have six calculations to choose from.

c. You must use the then-current 120% Midterm rate published by the IRS.

d. *You must continue taking distributions for 5 years or until age 59½,* **whichever is longer.**

e. You must document your calculations and save them until the end of the distribution period.

That's just the half of it. 72t calculations also involve locking yourself into a payment plan for at least 5 years – as mentioned in (d) above. And I mean locked. One mistake, one extra or missed payment in a year, and the entire calculation is voided – *and penalties taxes are due on every single distribution since Day-1.*

A 72t calculation can be your salvation. But it can also be your prison. I can't tell you how many times I've received calls from a client who is in year-3 of his distributions.

"I need more money for just this year," he says.

"But we've still got 2 years of distributions to go. You can't get any more money from the account," I reply.

"You don't understand. My (insert need here)

      a)   daughter is getting married
      b)   son is buying a house
      c)   wife wants a vacation home
      d)   buddy wants to sell me his Corvette

and I need some money from my account right away."

In many cases, we've made contingency plans for issues just like this. But what about the numerous people trying to do this themselves? Where are their contingency plans? Where are **your** contingency plans?

This is one of the biggest decisions you'll ever make. Even if you can do the calculation yourself, do you think that in the stress of an imminent retirement decision you'll make all the right choices?

If all of this sounds confusing, GOOD! It is. This isn't the time to be making decisions by the seat of your pants. If you don't know what you are doing, you can't possibly expect to make the best decision possible. And we haven't even dealt with the tax ramifications of retirement. (Which coincidentally is our next chapter.)

I've said it before, I'll probably say it again before you finish this book: You only get one shot at retirement. If you make a mistake, there is no going back to fix it when you are 70 or 75. It was far easier to retire 30 years ago than today. There were fewer decisions and less rules. This is no time to be making quick decisions based on little-to-no information or knowledge.

Tax Pitfalls!
The Biggest Drain On Your Income!

*I am proud to be paying taxes in the United States.
The only thing is -- I could be just as proud for half of the
money.*
Arthur Godfrey

Everyone hates income taxes, don't they? Sure we
pay them, but we never celebrate paying them. No one has a
party on April 15th. Heck, even the politicians and other
pundits that complain that we pay too little in taxes are never
there trying to pay more, are they?

I once had a client that complained for near an hour
about how the government didn't do enough to help folks
along and how it was due to the lack of tax collection. "We
need people to pay **MORE** in taxes, not less," he cried.
"People are really hurting out there!"

When I pointed out the few tax savings strategies that
we had implemented to save him money and how we could
reverse them, his tune changed instantly. Taxes were too low
– as long as someone else was paying them. He, like most
people, would like someone else to pay a lot in income taxes

while we find every loophole possible to pay the absolute minimum.

When it comes to retirement planning, taxes play a **HUGE** part. Every extra dollar saved is a dollar that you can spend. Save $1,000? You get an extra week in Florida avoiding the snow. Or maybe an extra dinner out every two weeks.

What's worse is that many people overpay their taxes every year. They just don't know the ins and outs of the tax code enough to help themselves.

Sadly, their accountants aren't much help either. A tax accountant typically looks at your tax information for **LAST** year to determine what can legally be done to reduce your tax liability. His focus is mostly looking for additional deductions to reduce your taxes.

He almost never looks at **THIS** year to see what lifestyle changes can be made to correct tax problems that crop up year after year. In fact, there are numerous ways to reduce your taxes without ever increasing your deductions.

For instance, let's say that you have an extra $5,000 in interest and dividend income annually and you never spend that money. You live off your wages or pension and Social Security. Year in and year out, you earn that $5,000 of reinvested interest and pay taxes on it.

What if you could continue receiving the interest, but make half of it tax-free or tax-deferred? Assuming a nominal federal bracket of 25% and a state tax of 5%, sheltering half of the income would *yield you an extra $750 per year!*

Boom! Just like that you got an extra $750 that Uncle was formerly taking from you. And if you got REAL aggressive and sheltered 80% of that money, you could cut your taxes by $1,200 annually.

Most of the individuals and accountants I've encountered would look at that $5,000 of interest income and pat themselves on the back for being so financially savvy as to have an extra $5,000 per year in income. They'd never look at the $750 or $1,200 they were losing. And in order to truly save money on your taxes, you need more than an accountant with a sharp pencil or the latest-and-greatest tax software. You need to be looking *ahead* to see what can be done today to save you money in taxes tomorrow.

Tax Problem #1: 20% Withholding Tax!

Back in 1992 – as we were coming out of the recession that began in 1987 – a new Pension and Profit Sharing rule came into effect – the 20% mandatory withholding tax.

This "tax" is not a tax, per se. It is a withholding. Just like fed, state, and FICA are withheld from your paycheck, the government wanted mandatory taxes withheld from any 401(k) or other "qualified" retirement plan.

As usual, Uncle wants his first. And I can't blame him. Back during the late 1980's recession, many executives received pink slips. Prior to 1993, you could take a full distribution from your 401(k) payable to yourself, and then you would have 60 days to roll that distribution to a new 401(k) or to a self-directed IRA. If you did not complete the rollover within the 60 days, the entire distribution was taxable to you.

Many of these executives took their distributions and "forgot" to roll them over. For many, the job prospects between 1987 and 1994 were slim. These executives lived on those former 401(k) plans. And come April 15 of the following year, Uncle came looking for his share. . .

And it wasn't there. The executive had spent it. All of it. As you can imagine, Uncle wasn't very happy.

So a new rule came into place in 1993. It said that if you took a distribution payable to yourself, the plan administrator would have to withhold 20% of the distribution amount and ship it to Uncle. Then they placed a mechanism in place to do a new "rollover" transaction where the cash would not touch your hands and you would be subject to no withholding and no penalties.

Seems fair, right?

WRONG!

What DID happen was that people, not understanding the new rules, still took distributions payable to themselves. And got a big surprise.

Let's say that you took a distribution of $100,000. Because of the complexity of the system, you accidentally requested the check be payable to you. Instead of getting $100,000, you would receive only $80,000.

How Do You Roll Over $100,000 If You Only Have $80,000?

The answer is – you dig deep in your OWN pocket for that extra $20,000. Because if you don't roll over the whole $100,000, count on the 20% being taxable to you – along with any associated penalties if you are under age 59½.

Can you see how serious this problem is? Think if you multiplied that problem by 5. Let's say you took a $500,000 distribution. Where are you going to get $100,000 to make up the rollover? At that point, it's practically impossible to fix.

Granted, over the last 25 years or so, education for investors has risen somewhat. But the option to take a distribution payable to yourself still exists – and I still see people trying to take distributions payable to themselves.

The forms used for 401(k) distributions aren't much help either. Sure, the information is there. But for someone who doesn't deal with this every day, it's a pile of legal mumbo-jumbo. I've seen 401(k) distribution forms that are 6 pages long. SIX PAGES!!!! All I want to do is transfer my money from ABC's 401(k) to Joe's House of Mutual Funds. Why do I need six pages to do so?

The government tries to help. And it's like the old joke of "I'm from the government and I'm here to help."

As part of this new law, the government requires everyone who received a distribution from a 401(k), 403(b) or other qualified plan to have received or had the opportunity to receive something called the *Special Tax Notice*.

Whether your distribution is done through a form or over the telephone with a 401(k) agent, they require you to acknowledge that you have received and read the *Special Tax Notice*.

It involves language like this from Fidelity's Special Tax Notice:

> *You may roll over to an employer plan all of a payment that includes after-tax contributions, but only through a direct rollover [and only if the receiving plan separately accounts for after-tax contributions and is not a governmental section 457(b) plan]. You can do a 60-day rollover to an employer plan of part of a payment that includes after-tax contributions, but only up to the amount of the payment that would be taxable if not rolled over. If you do a rollover of only a portion of*

the payment made to you, the nontax- able amounts are treated as being rolled over last.

Clear as mud! The average Special Tax Notice is 4-6 pages in length, single spaced and written (as you would expect) like an IRS Publication.

No, the government isn't going to help. If you are lucky, you will get a good 401(k) agent that will walk you through the transaction. Or not. I have done literally hundreds of these types of transactions in the past two decades and can tell you that frequently, I'm explaining how the plan works to the person on the other end of the receiver.

Tax Problem #2 - Distributions Prior to 59½!

We discussed at-length in the last chapter the complexities of taking a distribution prior to age 59½. I won't go into detail again on this issue. If you skipped the last chapter – shame on you. Go back and catch up. I'll wait for you.

There are severe tax ramifications related to the 72t calculation. As we discussed previously, any mistakes are compounded by the number of years you have taken distributions.

For example, let's say you retire at age 50 and start a 72t distribution from your 401(k) of $25,000 per year. At age 58, you decide to buy that piece of land in the mountains that you and your spouse have been looking at for years.

Setting up another 72t is impractical. You don't want to be locked into distributions for *another* five years. But wait. You have that small IRA at the bank. There's only $40,000 in it, but after taxes, it might be enough to make it all work.

Except for one little problem – the $40,000 distribution – even though it is from another separate account, nullifies your entire 72t calculation. Not only do you owe regular and penalty taxes on the $40,000 (possibly amounting to over $18,000), you will owe **BACK** penalties taxes for the last eight years – totaling another $20,000. So your $40,000 distribution netted you just $2,000.

That, as we say, is a **big** tax problem. Yet not the only problem. I see many people taking out 72t distributions who have no intention of using the money at all. They consider it a safety net. If they take out money every year, there's money building up in a taxable account for emergencies later.

While that seems sound, and in some cases **is** sound, most folks who do this are only costing themselves thousands in taxes for nothing. The problem has less to do with the distribution and more to do with everything else that is going on in their lives.

If someone is banking their 72t distribution, they probably have some sort of other income. That means the

72t income is what we call "marginal" income. That means it's taxed starting at your highest marginal bracket.

For many of us, that marginal bracket is 25%. Instead of paying some taxes in the zero-bracket, some in the 10% bracket, some in the 15% bracket and then some in the 25% bracket, the person that takes out "marginal" distributions starts right out at that 25% bracket.

By making a better plan regarding your future needs, you can avoid a needless distribution and paying thousands in unnecessary taxes. (More on tax brackets later in this chapter.)

Tax Problem #3 – Taxable Social Security Income!

Most folks know that if you receive Social Security (SS) income and work while between the ages of 62 and 66, you may see a reduction in benefits depending on how much you earn while working. A person can make about $16,000[iii] per year in wages before their SS checks drop – a dollar for every two dollars earned.

But what many don't realize is that Social Security may also be federally **income** taxable. And that's a kick in the pants because when Social Security was created, it was specifically excluded from taxable income. You cannot deduct your FICA contributions. In return, you were to receive your benefits tax free.

Then back in 1986, Senators Packwood and Rostenkowski created one of the most sweeping tax changes in the history of our country. Titled *The Tax Reform Act of 1986* or TRA86, it simplified much of the tax code. It also made some drastic changes like limiting deductions for interest paid. I know it was over 30 years ago, but I'm sure you remember deducting things like the interest on your car payment and credit card debt.

One other sweeping change in TRA86 was to make up to 50% of Social Security taxable for the *rich*. Who was defined as rich? An individual who had an income greater than $25,000 or a married couple with an income of more than $32,000.

And back in 1986, $32,000 was all the money in the world. If you could **work** and make $32,000 per year, you were on easy street. Few people, if any had a problem with retirees making more than that paying taxes on some of their Social Security.

Several years later during the Clinton administration, the folks in Washington updated the taxability of Social Security and made up to 85% taxable if your income exceeded $44,000. ($34,000 for single retirees.)

What few people realized in 1986 was that there was no Cost of Living increase to the tax thresholds. $32,000 in 1986 is the same $32,000 today. There has been no change.

Today, an average retiree that I meet with will easily receive more than $32,000 a year in income when you include pensions, interest, dividends, Social Security and IRA distributions. All of a sudden, *rich* is a relative term to mean *lots of retirees.*

This issue is **huge**. The ramifications are enormous.

- You pay taxes on income you expected to be tax-free.

- You have to either request that Social Security withhold taxes on your benefits or make quarterly tax payments.

- If you live in a income tax *piggy-back-state* like Rhode Island, your Social Security income is also taxed at the state level.

- Worst of all, **your federal income bracket has risen by leaps and bounds!**

What do I mean? How has your tax bracket changed? Let's look at two examples:

Assume you are in the 15% tax bracket and Social Security is just barely taxable. I mean, you are just barely over the limits to make a portion of your Social Security taxable.

For every dollar you receive in additional interest or dividends, fifty more cents of Social Security is taxable. That's how the calculation works.

In effect, you aren't in the 15% tax bracket, you are really in the **22.5% tax bracket!** (You pay 15% on the extra dollar you earned and 15% on the 50 cents of Social Security that just became taxable.) So extra income from a CD or increased dividend on your stock portfolio or another hour or two working costs you more than you anticipated.

And if you happen to be in the 25% tax bracket, your next dollar is no longer taxes at 25% but **at 46.25%!** (Remember, over $44,000, up to 85% of Social Security is taxable. So if you are in the 25% bracket, the odds are you will be taxed on up to 85%, not 50% of your Social Security.)

That means that when you add state income taxes, you could be paying **more than 50% in income taxes on each additional dollar earned!**

Unfortunately, there aren't too many ways to avoid this taxation. The tax form calculating the tax on Social Security includes any interest on tax-free investments you might have. Uncle Sam has thought of almost every loophole.

Almost.

But the best strategy is to have a tax plan!

Tax Problem #4 – Not Having A Tax Plan!

REAL LIFE STORY: How Saving A Few Dollars Can Cost You Thousands!

John and Linda have been retired for over a decade. I met them shortly after their daughter became a client. And up until I met with them, they handled all of their own finances. They filled out their own tax return. They managed their own investment portfolio.

But they wanted to talk to me because both of them realized they didn't have the time to keep an eye on all of these issues. There were grandchildren to spoil, trips to go on, and friends to visit with. John was spending many hours a week pouring over all of this financial data.

Back when he was working, this was never a problem. That's not to say that John had lost his edge when he retired. Quite the contrary. John keeps me on my toes at every meeting.

But back when John was actively employed, financial life was definitely simpler. With the myriad of new investment products, endless tax code changes, and economic ups and downs, John just didn't feel they could keep up.

John and Linda had a sound plan for retirement. In reality, they were unlikely to run out of money before they passed on. But they wanted to make the most of every dollar. They knew that every dollar wasted was one that they could have spent or could have left for their children.

One thing that John did was take a sizeable annual distribution from his former employer's 401(k) plan. What's sizeable? How about $60,000?

"John, that's a lot to take out of your plan annually. Do you use all of that?" I asked.

"Well," John mused. "Probably most of it. Whatever I don't use I usually put into my brokerage account."

I thought for a moment. "John, just how much is **in** the brokerage account?"

"About $500,000."

I nearly choked. John and Linda were taking *TAXABLE* distributions from John's

401(k) while they had a wealth of non-taxable assets they could tap.

We made some adjustments to John and Linda's distributions, dropping it to less than half of what it used to be. When they needed extra money, they tapped the brokerage account. But that was fairly infrequent since we saved **over $13,000 in income taxes.**

Quick Tax Tip: Know Your Tax Bracket?

John and Linda are an extreme, yet real, example of not having a tax plan. If you take money from whatever account you want, whenever you feel like it, you are likely paying Uncle Sam way too much.

Probably the most important piece of information you need in order to fight the tax ogre is your tax bracket. One of the complexities of the US Tax Code is that our income tax is progressive. The more you make, the larger percentage of your income the government takes.

And with all of the tax changes in the last five to ten years, it is difficult to keep track of what bracket you are in and what the next one looks like.

Currently, our federal tax bracket starts at 10% and reaches a maximum tax of 39.6%. And if you are like most people I encounter, you are thinking, *"Ten percent!?!?!? There's a ten percent bracket?"*

It's fairly small. The first $9,000-18,000 of income is taxed at this bracket. Most of us shoot right through it. And most of us never even **see** the 39.6% tax bracket for incomes over about $465,000. It's just too high for all but the "1%'ers" to encounter.

But why does your tax bracket matter? It tells you how much money you lose in taxes for every extra dollar earned. A person in a 10% bracket may spend days looking for a $100 deduction to save only $10 in taxes. That's probably a poor use of their time.

By contrast, someone who is in a high tax bracket – especially when combined with state income taxes – can reap huge rewards. That same $100 tax deduction could be worth $30, $40, and possibly even $50!

For instance, many tax-free investments are geared towards higher tax bracket individuals. In many cases, lower-bracket folks are **losing money** investing in these vehicles.

Let me give you a fictitious example. Let's say that a certain municipal bond is paying 4% interest. And a taxable CD or bond is paying 5.5%. I've known many people in the 10% or 15% tax bracket that would rather buy the municipal bond paying 4% because it is tax free. *Tax Free* just sounds better, doesn't it? Like *Buy One Get One Free*?

Let's assume we have 2 investors, one in the 35% bracket and one in the 10% bracket. Each invests $10,000.

First, let's look at the high tax bracket investor.

Taxable Bond
$10,000 investment
$550.00 interest (5.5%)
-192.50 taxes (35% tax)
$357.50 After Taxes

Tax Free Bond
$10,000 investment
$400.00 interest (4%)
NO TAXES (tax free)
$400.00 After Taxes

Now let's look at the 10% bracket investor

Taxable Bond
$10,000 investment
$550.00 interest (5.5%)
- 55.00 taxes (10% tax)
$495.00 After Taxes

Tax Free Bond
$10,000 investment
$400.00 interest (4%)
NO TAXES (tax free)
$400.00 After Taxes

Clearly, the low-tax-bracket investor is better off actually *PAYING* the taxes.

It's not important to just pay the minimum in taxes. It's important to put the maximum back in your pocket – even if that means putting some in Uncle's pocket as well.

Once you know your tax bracket, you can then plan where to get the money you need to spend. John and Linda were in the 28% tax bracket and almost hitting the (at the time) 31% tax bracket. That meant tax planning was VERY serious.

I have met other people who, while they had a sizeable portfolio, were still in the 15% tax bracket. Their tax strategies were far different than most of their wealthy peers.

How you receive every single dollar is critical. As I stated at the beginning of this chapter, every dollar you save in taxes is another that you are allowed to spend.

Pulling It All Together!

Tax planning is one of the most difficult and the most rewarding areas of my practice. It's where things are complicated, but the benefits are tangible and, as in the case of John and Linda, meaningful.

But tax planning takes a lot of time and effort. I won't lie to you. The rules for IRA's alone fill volumes. I have one book – ONE BOOK – in my office relating just to IRA tax rules. It totals over 900 pages, not including tax reference tables.

Add to that the specific rules relating to 401(k) plans, 403(b) plans, SIMPLE-IRA's, pensions, capital gains, dividends, Social Security and a hundred other items you might encounter. All of it adds up to a pile of information.

Tax planning isn't a part-time job. But the dividends can be huge. It might be in your best interest to have someone review your tax situation – not just your returns, but your entire situation – to see how much extra you are giving Uncle Sam annually.

Risk – The Secret Retirement Killer!

RISK!

Just reading the word makes your pulse quicken. I hate risk. I'm pretty sure you do too.

When I think of risk, I think of riding the Space Shuttle. Or testing a new nuclear submarine. Or going bungee jumping. Those are risky activities and I don't do any of them.

When we talk about investing, the word *risk* crops up. Even faster than the word *return*. When you discuss the two, it's risk and return, not return and risk. We think about the risk of an investment before even discussing its return.

Risk is defined as loss. In statistical terms, risk is fluctuation. Up and down are defined within risk. But we don't care about ups, do we? We care about downs. An investment you bought yesterday for $10 is now selling for $5. That's risk! But if it's selling for $20, that's not risk, it's a reflection of your stock-picking genius!

And as you see, most people think of downward fluctuation as risk. And if I were to poll 100 people, the vast majority would probably say that the investment arena with the most risk is the stock market. That's because of the way we define risk.

Hidden Risk – The Secret Killer!

Let me tell you about my grandmother. She was a wonderful woman. She raised five children while my grandfather worked for years for the Railroad. In the late 70's, he retired with a small savings account plus his Railroad Retirement. And in the early 1980's, he died of emphysema.

Shortly thereafter, all of the *kids* got together and realized that Nanna couldn't take care of the family homestead for much longer. She had received a reasonable income from Grampy's retirement, plus if she sold the house, she'd have a sizable nest egg. While she wouldn't be swimming in money, she'd be doing well enough on her "fixed income."

That was 1984 or so. Twenty years later, we prepared to celebrate Nanna's 90th birthday. And she's no longer *doing well enough.* In fact, things are very tight. That "fixed income" from the Railroad was embarrassingly low. And because of it, the nest egg she had from selling her home hadn't grown, but has dwindled to help make ends meet.

66

What happened? Why was Nanna having such a hard time making ends meet?

- Because the cost to fill her pantry more than doubled in the 20 years after my Grandfather passed away

- Because her rent went up on a regular basis. In fact, Nanna had to move because of issues relating to rent.

- Because medication was more expensive. And she was taking far more pills than she did 20+ years earlier.

- Because life in general was more expensive than it was in 1984. And it's definitely more expensive today than when she turned 90 over a decade ago.

The true reason why she struggled is because of a risk she never even considered: *Inflation.*

When we think of inflation, we hearken back to the 1970's, when gas prices, and subsequently everything else, skyrocketed in price. We don't think of it as something we deal with today.

But remember your childhood. Think of what an ice cream cone cost. I know you remind your grandkids how much it cost "back in the day." A dime? Maybe a quarter, tops? Well, when I was a boy, it was a dollar. And that was in the 1970's. Today? Ice cream cones at an ice cream shop will run you $4 or more.

FOUR BUCKS FOR AN ICECREAM CONE!?!?!?!?!

That's inflation. It's not limited to a specific period in time like the 70's. It happens year-in and year-out. In fact, if you look at inflation tables from 1984 to 2014, the annual rate of inflation was over 5% in only one year. Just one. And in only about a half-dozen years was it over 4%.[iv]

But all those little inflations added up so that Nanna couldn't afford to do much of anything anymore.

It's hard to consider inflation even a risk. It isn't a "maybe" or a "sometimes."

Inflation is inevitable. The only other option is to have prices falling – or deflation. That is so destructive to the economy, the government just about kills itself to avoid that ever happening. And we haven't seen significant deflation since the 1930's.

The government has two choices: Inflation or deflation. Since inflation is less destructive, it strives for a controlled inflationary economy – somewhere between 2 and 4% inflation annually. But I'm getting off track.

As I was saying, inflation is inevitable. It isn't truly a risk because we **KNOW** it will occur. It's just a question of how bad it will be year-to-year. And in the long run of retirement, the highs and the lows will probably even out.

The risk is that *"fixed income"* investments will lose their value over time. How? Because after taxes and inflation, sometimes we are left with less than we started.

Let's assume you have a $50,000 CD paying you 3%. In addition, let's assume you are the 20% tax bracket (federal and state). Finally, assume that inflation this year was 2.5%. Now take a look at how our investment faired.

$50,000 CD paying 3%
Income $1,500
(less) Taxes   -300
(less) Inflation -1,250   *(This is how much less your $50,000 is worth because of inflation.)*
Equals: ($50)

In case you are unsure, those parentheses around the $50 means you *lost* $50 for every $50,000 you invested. What if that happened year-in and year-out for 20 or 30 years? Yes, it may not appear that you've lost any money in that CD, but you can't buy half the stuff you used to with the principal that is left.

"So what?" you are thinking. "How much could inflation affect my retirement? Even if I'm losing $50 per year, I can last a lot of years. I probably won't live that long."

Fortunately (or unfortunately) you are wrong. The odds are that you will spend at least 30 years in *retirement.* My grandmother was retired for about 30 years and she struggled for at least 10 of those years. What is going to happen to you if you live that long? Do you want to ration your money in the last decade of your life?

Medical science gets better every day. I read an article several years ago that a 65 year old is projected to live 25 years. Odds are you haven't even **turned** 65 yet nor do you expect to work until 65. It won't be surprising to see people living 40 or 45 years in retirement. Given long life expectancies and people's penchant for retiring early, you could live more of your adult-life in retirement than you spent working.

And in that time span, inflation is serious. At a 4% clip, the cost of goods will double every 17 years. That means if you are on a fixed pension, you will only be able to buy a quarter of the stuff you buy now in 34 years. That's a huge problem. Couple that with your dwindling CD's in real "inflation-adjusted" dollars and you are behind the biggest 8-ball you've ever seen.

Solving The Problem

In the equation above, there are only two factors we have influence over: Taxes and Rate of Return. We can't control inflation. We can't control how much money we have once we retire (unless you win the lottery). So we can either overcome the taxes, or use higher returns to overcome the inflation.

SOLUTION #1 – OVERCOME THE TAXES!

As we discussed in the last chapter, controlling taxes goes a long way towards increasing your purchasing power. Every dollar you save in taxes is another one you get to spend.

There are two basic tax reduction strategies available to us: Tax Free and Tax Deferred. Tax free we discussed in the last chapter. Sometimes, if your bracket is high enough, it can be advantageous. But tax-free investments usually pay lower rates of returns which, in turn, reduces your after-tax earnings.

But what about tax deferred? What is it? Basically your IRA and 401(k) are tax deferred. You don't pay taxes on the income of these investments until you actually withdraw and spend the money.

I will tell you a secret. I hate taxes. OK, you probably already figured that out. But here's the one that really gets me riled up. I hate paying taxes on money that I didn't get to spend.

If I have an investment that makes me $1,000 per year and I reinvest that income, I don't think it's fair that Uncle Sam gets to tax me on that money. With a nominal 25% federal income tax and a 5% state income tax, I have to fork over $300 in additional taxes for the *privilege* of investing and earning that $1,000. That's not fair.

I'm sure you don't think it's fair either, but you probably never thought about it in that light. And I can show you two places to look to see how much Uncle Sam is squeezing you for. If you look on your Form 1040 that you filed last April, you'll notice two lines on the first page. They say something like *Interest Income* and *Ordinary Dividends.* That's that money that you are likely reinvesting, yet Uncle taxes you on it anyway.

Let's use that same $50,000 CD we discussed earlier. I find that most people who have this problem tend to have an interest problem rather than a dividend problem. So let's focus there.

In our example, the CD earned $1,500 per year and we paid $300 in taxes. But what if we eliminated that $300? But what type of investment is appropriate? We can't dump more money into our 401(k). And IRA limitations will only allow about $5,500 to be contributed. What investment can we use to invest $50,000 and defer the taxes right away?

Use of Annuities

In most instances, you can use some sort of fixed annuity. What is a fixed annuity? Think of it as a CD issued by an insurance company. It has a stated rate for a stated time period. But because it's issued by an insurance company, we don't have to pay taxes on the interest until we withdraw it. I'm oversimplifying things a bit, but this is basically how fixed annuities work. *(I'll explain some pitfalls of using annuities in a minute.)*

So let's re-run that scenario again using a fixed annuity instead of a taxable CD:

$50,000 Fixed Annuity paying 3%

Income	$1,500
(less) Taxes	-0
(less) Inflation	-1,250
Equals:	$250

While $250 doesn't set the world on fire, we are keeping ahead of inflation. We are maintaining our purchasing power. And for someone who is averse to the stock market, this is an excellent solution.

Annuity Pitfalls

While fixed annuities are great for many people, they aren't for everyone. I find many people who have them that shouldn't. Why? Because they are an easy sell for a sharp insurance salesman. You see it for yourself above. Saving a pile in taxes is everyone's dream.

But be careful. You might be meeting up with someone who is seeing dollar signs – for him, not you. Be sure to understand everything about your contract. Some contracts are practically impossible to get out of. Other times, there is a big *come-on* or *bonus* rate in year one which drops considerably below what CD's are paying in years two and beyond. In other situations, you might be investing with an insurance company with less than stellar ratings.

Annuities can be "slam-dunks" to increase your overall return, but selecting the right annuity for your situation isn't. Always be careful.

SOLUTION #2 – OVERCOME THE INFLATION!

The only other area you can control in the equation is the return above and beyond inflation. And here we come back to that discussion on risk and the stock market. Trading one risk for another.

There are few ways to consistently beat inflation other than investing in stocks. It's just that simple. Over time, the stock market gives you a higher return for the "risk" you take by investing in it.

From 1926 until 2014, the stock market returned approximately 10.1% per year. Inflation grew at 2.9% and short-term Treasury Bills earned about 3.5%. [v] On average, the stock market made over 7% more than inflation annually. That is substantial.

Yet it isn't a cake-walk to invest in the stock market. We can't just invest each year and earn 10.1% can we? If we could, inflation wouldn't be a problem, would it?

So how do we do it? What's involved? Let me start out by telling you another quick story:

Back while I was in college, I worked for a trust company writing small computer programs to do calculations and track financial information for their clients.

At the time, I really didn't know a whole lot about the stock market. So I spent as much time as I could get away with in the *trading room*. The trust officers were always coming in and out. The two traders were always on the phone. If I could learn about how to make money in the stock market, this was the place.

There was one trader named Tom who seemed to do a ton of work. He'd come in an hour early for work. He'd use one of the two personal computers the firm had. (Back then, PC's were just becoming useful for business. It's strange to talk of having to get in line to use a PC at a billion-dollar investment firm, but we did.)

Tom did analysis from the moment he got in until the opening bell at 9:30. Then he went to work in the trading room while refining his data to present to the trust officers for recommendations. He took his work very seriously.

A few times, I'd be in early and catch him on the PC. He'd go over this chart or graph and talk about when a stock "got pregnant," his slang for dropping like a rock. This was around 1987 so a lot of stocks were "getting pregnant."

To me, Tom was the man to know. He HAD to have amassed millions by now – even on his trader's salary. So I asked him one day: *"Tom, how do you make a million dollars in the stock market?"*

Tom leaned back in his swivel-chair and said,

"Start With Two Million Dollars!"

Tom, in many ways, was right. Investing in the stock market, as we've discussed, can be a crap-shoot from year to year. Especially in the last decade or so. But what if I told you the stock market was more of a sure thing than you thought?

Let me show you some facts beyond that 10.1% number I quoted earlier. These are facts, not my opinion.

The graph below shows the individual-year returns for the S&P500 Stock Market Index from 1926 to 2014.

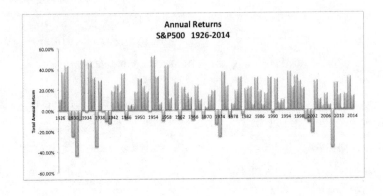

As you can see, there were some pretty ugly years in there. In fact, 24 out of 89 years – or about three out of every 10 years – you saw a loss. That's not very good odds for short-term investing.

A few years ago, I got a call from a client. His credit card company is foolishly willing to lend him up to $30,000, interest-free for the next 12 months. He was wondering if we could invest that money and MAKE money on the credit card company's money.

"Sure!" I said. "We can put it in an 11 month CD and make about one percent or almost $300."

"Yeah, but could we invest it in the stock market?"

"We could. We've got almost a one-in-three chance you can lose money on this deal. Are you willing to lose, say 10% or $3,000?"

He didn't want to do that. I don't blame him. That's too much risk, right?

But what if we changed the game a bit? Let's say we invest for a longer term. Say 15 years.

"Fifteen Years?" you are thinking. Yes, fifteen years. In reality, this isn't a very long time. It's probably less than half the time you will be retired. It's definitely less than half of your working life. So let's look at those returns

if we had held the same S&P 500 Stock Market Index for 15 years.

Now we're looking at a nice graph. In the past 64 15-year periods, the S&P500 Stock Market Index has lost money just once – the period beginning right before the Great Depression through 1943.

NOTE: This is by no means an implied guarantee that the stock market will never lose money in a 15-year period. As I'm sure you understand, past performance is no barometer of future returns. In addition, you CAN lose money even when the stock market as a whole is rising if you invest in a bad company or purchase a bad mutual fund.

All of a sudden, we leapfrog this inflation problem, don't we? The longer we invest in the stock market, the more we get ahead of inflation.

So Why Do People Lose Money In The Stock Market?

I'm sure that's what you are thinking. In fact, if you are the average investor, you are *really* thinking, "Why can't I make any money in the stock market?"

The reason is we don't like risk. When stocks are down, are you likely to invest? We've already seen from the first chart that even in the darkest of times, the stock market has come back. So when stocks are down, it's the best time to invest, right?

How many people bought Chrysler back in 1981? Not many. We don't like investing when things are bad.

Conversely, how many inexperienced investors jumped on the technology bandwagon in 1999, only to see a 40% drop in their accounts within 3 years? Why would you buy after years of record returns? Why invest at the top?

Our human nature causes us to sell low and buy high. We get caught up in the frenzy and just follow the crowd – right off the nearest cliff.

I won't even discuss the late-1990's day-traders who lost everything. Not just a few day traders. Virtually all of them. The vast majority of these folks lost *every dollar they invested* in day trading. Not just a 30% loss or a 50% loss. They experienced, by and large, a 100% loss.

How Can You Avoid It?

The best way to avoid making bad investment decisions is to have an investment plan and stick to it. Good, bad, or otherwise, you need to stay on your plan. It doesn't matter what the stock market is doing day to day or even over the course of a single year or two.

What matters is investing for the long-haul. And then sticking to that plan. I've seen many people lose significant amounts of money because they deviated from their plans. Some gave up when the market was down. And then kicked themselves when the market came back.

Others walked away from their investment plan in the late 90's to pursue the "gigantic returns" of technology stocks. And they got wiped out doing it.

If your plan is sound and your investments are sound, there are very few reasons to deviate from that plan ever. I don't have the space in this book to discuss how to develop an investment plan. There are a multitude of books on the subject – many of them available at your local library. Or you can hire an investment advisor.

Either way, you need to find that plan and stick to it. Because the risk of inflation is real and it's happening to your money *right now!* And as we've seen, there are only two solutions: Beat the taxes or beat the rate of inflation. Or best of all: Beat both.

Long Term Care!
The Latest Threat To Retirement!

Probably the most recent issue facing retirees – and one of the most serious – is *Long Term Care*. In part because we live longer and in part because of conditions that just didn't exist 100 years ago. People are more in need of some sort of medical *support* later in retirement, be that in a nursing home, assisted living facility, or some sort of home care provided by a skilled health care worker, spouse, or child.

Failing to plan, even in part, for a long term care stay is one of the biggest mistakes a retiree can make. The type of care needed is expensive and can quickly strip your life savings away from you.

Long Term Care is a new concept to many Americans. Historically, human beings have "taken care of their own." It was not unusual for a family to have several generations living under one roof. The odds are good that your parents cared for an elderly relative in their home.

And if you asked most older retirees today, the odds are the last place they'd want to be in their golden years is living in their children's homes.

Attitudes have changed. People delight in, and even vehemently defend, their independence. Ever since the economic boom in the 1940's, families have been moving out to suburbia. The concept of a family home, lived in by many generations, is becoming an anachronism. Most older couples enjoy living on their own in their own home – and the younger generations have grown accustomed their way of life as well. You gained independence. So did they.

And neither of you is likely to give it up.

When I ask clients for their thoughts regarding their care as they get older, I hear one response time and time again: **"I do not want to be a burden on my children."**

This can be a wonderful idea. Independence is important to all of us, and maintaining that independence in your later years is even more vital for someone who can hold onto the familiarity of their surroundings.

It can also lead to problems. Independent living can literally be an accident waiting to happen.

Sometimes, seniors have a hard time letting go of their independence. This leads to not getting *any* help when it's needed. And fairly often, we find elderly residents entering a nursing home or assisted living facility because they became injured in a home that was dangerous or detrimental to their condition.

Most younger retirees between 50 and 70 are vaguely aware that decisions need to be made regarding their future once they become "elderly." Most are reluctant to do anything because those decisions involve relinquishing some control over their financial assets, their property, and their decision-making abilities.

So what's the answer? There are countless solutions. Let's start by understanding the "system" surrounding Long Term Care.

A Long Term Care Primer

When discussing long term care, there is almost a second language that must be learned. It's sort of like talking to a 20-something about technology. All those words *sound* serious, but we have no idea what they mean. Let's take some time to get you acclimated to this new language.

Facility Care

By definition, if you are being cared for *outside* your home, you are receiving facility care. This doesn't mean someplace you go for the day. It means this is your new home – either temporarily or permanently.

The first thought that comes to your mind is ***nursing home.*** And at one time, that's exactly what Facility Care encompassed. A nursing home.

No one likes nursing homes. In fact, we all hate them. We hate visiting them. We have nightmares of having to put a relative – or ourselves into one. Yet nursing homes

are full. Why? Because at some point, some people get so sick that they need hospital-like care 24/7.

Assisted Living

In recent years, there has been a new form of Facility Care called Assisted Living Facilities. Originally, the designers of these residences were planning on retirees aged 65-79 to move here to "get away from it all." Meals, usually gourmet-chef prepared, are provided. There is no lawn to cut, no water heater to fix, no snow to shovel. And virtually everything is provided through one monthly fee.

For someone who had little choice other than a nursing home 20 years ago, an Assisted Living Facility provides a mix of independence and skilled care. Each person receives a private room with a kitchenette. They have 24/7 emergency care, and an activities program that would exhaust a 4 year old.

Home Care

Home care is exactly what it sounds like. Care in **your** home. This can range from your spouse or child to a skilled worker who comes in as often as every day.

The one misconception of home care is that you can receive 24/7 care at your home. Well, I guess you can – provided your last name is Rockefeller. Typically, Home Care provides a skilled worker for a 4 or 8 hour shift.

In all types of care, the help received is called *custodial care.* These are not licensed nurses or aides.

These are usually trained, skilled custodial workers who aid in the day-to-day living needs of the patients. Needs such as eating, bathing, dressing and getting around. These custodial care workers cannot administer medicine nor provide medical treatment. You CAN hire registered nurses to care for you – but again, only if your name is Rockefeller.

Who Pays?

The cost of Long Term Care seems to be constantly rising. Below is a list of the types of care we discussed and the average cost. It doesn't take long before these start biting into your retirement nest egg.

Nursing Home $128,000/year
Assisted Living $62,000/year
Home Care $55,000/year
(Average Costs as of 2016.)

It may have taken you *years* to accumulate your first $120,000 in savings. It will be spent in a one-year stay at a nursing home. This problem is **serious.**

If we break down the pie chart of who pays, it comes out like this:

Who Pays For Long Term Care?

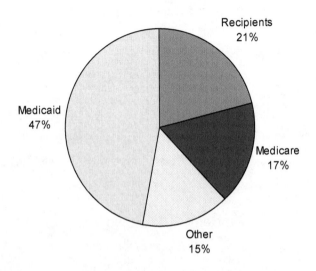

Individual recipients pay about 21% of the total bill. Another 17% is paid by Medicare and 15% is paid for in other ways such as by a relative, private insurance or other programs. **That means that *almost half* of the long term care costs in this country are borne by the Medicaid system.**[vi]

Medicare vs. Medicaid

Two little letters. That's all that separates MedicaID and MedicaRE. But their purpose is vastly different.

Medicare is the primary health insurance vehicle for virtually everyone over the age of 65. Even if you have other health insurance, that coverage seamlessly integrates with Medicare without you even noticing it.

Medicare covers medical costs. Doctors, hospitals, nurses, blood, tests, therapy, etc., It does **NOT** typically pay for custodial care. Let me say that again, Medicare does not typically pay for custodial care.

"But I heard that Medicare will pay the first 100 days of a nursing home stay!" you claim. Well, that is half-true. Maybe even a quarter true. Here is what Medicare requires in order to pay for a nursing home stay:

- A person must be hospitalized for at least 3 consecutive days, not counting the day of discharge.
- A person must be admitted to the nursing home within 30 days of discharge.
- The services provided relate to the condition for which they were hospitalized.
- They require skilled nursing services or rehabilitation on a daily basis.
- The doctor ordering the care certifies at the time of admission that the patient needs skilled care on a daily basis, plus certifies this need on day 14, and every 30 days thereafter.
- Medicare will pay 100% of the cost for the first 20 days. For the remaining 80 days, the patient must satisfy a $158 copay (approximately $9,000 for the total stay.)
- **If the patient ceases to improve, or "plateaus," payment by Medicare stops immediately!**[vii]

The chances of most people's nursing home stays meeting those seven requirements is pretty slim. Even if Medicare pays all that it should, you still end up paying over $12,600 in the first 100 days.

And it is unlikely that Medicare will continue paying for all 100 days.

Let's say you have a stroke. You are in the hospital for 5 days and then are transferred to a nursing home for care and rehabilitation (fulfilling all of the requirements for Medicare to pay for your nursing home stay). Forty-four days later, your doctor and physical therapist come in and say, "Mr. Jones, you are doing well, but you haven't improved in the last 7 days. I think this is the best we're going to do."

Not only are you crushed by that diagnosis, the next thing your doctor does is notify Medicare, which denies any future claims. You are not better, you won't get better, and now you have to figure out how to pay for it all. This isn't a pleasant place to be.

Medicaid

As I mentioned earlier, the most prolific payer of Long Term Care bills is Medicaid. It's also known under other names such as MassHealth in Massachusetts and MediCal in California.

Medicaid was designed to be the health insurer of those who were unable to insure themselves. The unemployed, the destitute, and every child in America who does not have other insurance. (Even before the Affordable Care Act!) Contrary to what you hear on TV, those most in need do get health care – provided by this joint program between Uncle Sam and the states.

Medicaid is a strange program. It is primarily funded through federal money, yet each state controls how and where that money is spent. It's a conglomeration of state laws founded on federal rules – both of which change about as often as the tax code.

The most active rule-changing area relates to nursing homes and long term care. The system was designed to pay for nursing home care for those who were too poor to pay for themselves. Over time, people figured out ways of making themselves *appear* poor to qualify. So the government changed the rules. And the people found more strategies. And the government changed the rules again. And so it goes on today.

Medicaid will not pay for any type of care less than full nursing home care. So anyone planning on using Medicaid to pay their Long Term Care needs can only have those needs met in one place: The nursing home.

States will use a set of complicated formulas to determine a person's nursing home eligibility. Most relate to assets. Other than one vehicle and a home, a single person is allowed to have no more than a couple of thousands of dollars in assets. In addition, virtually all of their Pension and Social Security income is attached to pay for their care.

Married couples have it a *bit* easier. They can keep up to about $120,000 in financial assets, plus the **community spouse** (i.e.: the one staying at home) can keep all of his or her own income. If that income places the spouse under the poverty level, they can also petition to keep some of the patient's income. But this is very complicated and requires a lawyer to plead your case in court.

In either case, relying on Medicaid will bankrupt a family. This probably isn't **that** serious for a single person. Once you have exhausted your assets at a nursing home, the odds of you getting better and leaving to live a normal life are fairly slim.

But this can be devastating to a married couple. A husband goes into a nursing home and within a few years, the wife is virtually bankrupted with nowhere to turn.

Gifting, Your Home, and Abracadabra!

In the past, many people have tried to gift away assets before they enter a nursing home. Currently, if you gift assets within 60 months of entering a facility, they will more than likely disqualify you from receiving Medicaid for a length of time.

Does this mean giving your grandson $50 or even $500 for his birthday will disqualify you? No. But significant gifts made within that 5 year window can cause you to be disqualified from a few months to indefinitely – depending on the size of the gift.

Let me give you an example. Let's say you give your grandson $50,000 to pay for his college education. Fifty-eight months later, you are in a nursing home and are applying for Medicaid.

As a side note – the Medicaid application process is a daunting one. You fill out a large application then provide 60 months of financial data. Do you have 60 months of statements and records? I know I don't. And then Medicaid goes over it with a fine-tooth comb. If you missed anything, you won't get a request for clarification, you will get a denial notice. This is important to know.

Fifty-eight months later, you are filling out this massive application and disclose the $50,000 gift almost five years ago. Medicaid responds by telling you that even though the money was given for his education and it was a long time ago, *you are disqualified from any Medicaid payments for the next six months!*

That's a sudden change. That money that no longer exists has now come back to bite you.

Protecting Your Home

The biggest asset most folks have is their home. And Medicaid allows you to keep your home for your lifetime. But if you receive benefits from Medicaid, they **will** place a lien on your home and possibly own it by the time you pass on. So many strategies regarding gifting before you need care revolve around giving your home to your children.

All I can tell you is to be careful. Once you do not own your home, all sorts of problems can erupt. For instance,

- The child who now owns your home *could* get divorced – and you could get evicted.
- Your child may get sued – and a lien can be placed on your home, forcing a sale.
- Your child may get into financial difficulty and your home may be seized to pay the judgment.

In all these cases, you can be thrown out of your own home. Because it's no longer yours, you have no rights to live there. Gifting your home is possible. But you should be aware of the dangers.

One final strategy I see being foisted on unsuspecting people is the purchase of annuities. I will not go into detail regarding this strategy except to say this: If it was such a massive loophole, don't you think the government would have closed it by now? Annuity strategies can seem like magic, but they are dangerous, irrevocable and tend to ensure you lose some of your money, if not most of it. Unless you have special circumstances, avoid Medicaid annuity strategies.

What's On The Horizon?

Odds are, nothing significant is on the horizon. With the Affordable Care Act and the relative stability of length-of-nursing-home stays at about 3 years, it is unlikely that major changes to the Medicaid laws are coming in the next several years.

Alas, Medicaid continues to be a huge problem. It is approaching a half of a trillion dollars in spending per year. Most of that is on health insurance for lower income Americans.

Government is expensive. And they are always looking for places to cut. This is one of those places. If we do see changes to Medicaid, expect it to get worse, not better.

Long Term Care Insurance – Private Industry To The Rescue!

With all the gyrations of Medicaid planning, it still boils down to one thing: In order to receive Medicaid assistance, you **MUST** receive care in a nursing home. There is no Medicaid strategy that will hide your assets and pay for a home health aide. Nor to make your house disappear and allow you to enter an Assisted Living Facility.

There is but one strategy, short of paying the bill out of your own pocket, that will pay for virtually any type of care: Long Term Care Insurance (LTCI).

LTCI provides income to you to pay your long term care bills should you become ill or incapacitated. *YOU* get to decide where and how that care is provided. If you want to stay home *and that is medically feasible,* you can stay home. If you want assisted living, you can have assisted living.

Keep in mind the insurance companies best interest coincide with yours. You don't want to leave your home – and that is the cheapest option available to the insurance company. They won't argue if you want to spend less of their money.

How LTCI Works

There are many *bells and whistles* that you can add, but virtually all policies have some basic benefits and features.

Each policy will have a stated **Daily Benefit.** This is the maximum amount the policy will pay *per day* for your care. It can range from as little as $50 per day up to several hundred. In addition, there is a maximum **Benefit Period.** This can be expressed two ways – in dollars or in days.

If the Benefit Period is denoted in dollars, that's the pool of money you have to draw from before benefits run out. (Like virtually all forms of health insurance, LTCI has a cap.) If it is denoted in days, it expresses how long a policy will last if you maximize the daily benefit every day. For instance, a policy that pays $200 per day for 4 years may last 8 years if you only use $100 per day in benefits.

There is also an **Elimination Period** on each policy. This means that you will have to satisfy some sort of deductible – expressed in days of care – before benefits are paid. Elimination Periods range from zero days up to 90, 180, and is some cases 360 days.

Other Key Benefits

On all policies, there is some sort of **Inflation Protection**. This can be calculated three different ways:

1. No inflation protection
2. 5% Simple Interest
3. 5% Compound Interest

None means none. This is by far the cheapest alternative. But someone buying LTCI at age 65 or younger will need some sort of inflation protection to allow the policy to keep pace with the ever-increasing cost of care.

If you select inflation protection, you can decide between simple or compound interest. Just like a CD at the bank, compound interest is better – but this benefit again comes at a higher price. In some policies, the compound benefit increase rider is almost 50% of the premium. For someone in their 70's, that may be impractical. But someone in their 50's may see it as a big advantage.

Some policies offer a **Return Of Premium** rider. This means that if you don't use the benefits, your heirs will receive the full amount of your premiums back at your death. This can be an attractive option, but it often doubles the cost of coverage.

Other plans offer a **Single Premium** option. This just means you make one large payment instead of paying yearly. Problems can arise if you die early and never use the benefit. Typically, this plan is coupled with the Return of Premium rider.

Finally, some plans offer payments through an **Indemnity Rider.** This can appear to be a goldmine. Effectively, the plan says that if you are in need of care, they will send you up to the daily maximum every day to do whatever you wish. You can spend the money on care – or go to the casino.

This isn't some sort of lottery where we cheer when we get sick. LTCI is designed to give you choices in your care while preserving your assets and income for your spouse and children. It isn't about cashing in. Indemnity plans can be very dangerous and tend to be oversold as some sort of investment. Beware.

Other Considerations

Keep in mind that LTCI is a form of health insurance. This means the premiums are *NOT* guaranteed for life.

Some plans offer a guarantee period but no one offers a lifetime guaranteed premium.

Does that mean you should expect the premiums to rise in the future? Maybe. It depends on many things. A company that is offering a too-good-to-be-true premium may hit you with increases later on. Or a company that is very liberal in accepting new customers may experience more claims than expected – and increase premiums.

While the LTCI industry has been around for over 4 decades, the changes that continue to occur within the senior demographic add a certain level of uncertainty to every policy.

What's The Cost?

LTCI is expensive. I won't lie to you. If you purchase LTCI and never use it, it will be the most expensive thing you have ever wasted money on. It's literally money thrown out the window.

And it's expensive if you don't have it – and need care. Unfortunately, we don't have a crystal ball to see who will need care and who won't.

Your best bet is to have a plan designed for you – something that is ideal for your situation – and then find out the price. That's the only way to see what is affordable *to you.*

Too many agents find out what you are willing to pay and design a plan around that. That just ensures you to get the wrong insurance – often inadequate in many areas. You need to explore your **needs** first, then you can decide what benefits to look into.

If you do need care, LTCI can be the best investment in the world. As we said above, it will pay for many different types of care. You get to retain full control over **how and where** you receive your care.

REAL LIFE STORY: Success and Failure With Long Term Care

Fred and Donna don't know Chuck and Sue, but they could. They are about the same age today – mid 70's. And their situations are fairly similar. They both have an above-average retirement nest egg. They each own one well-priced home. And they each have had concerns about Long Term Care.

About four years ago, Fred and Donna brought up their concerns to me in our first meeting. "We don't want to have any problems or lose any money if we get sick," Fred told me.

As we explored the issue, both Fred and Donna expressed concern that if either one of them got sick, the other would live in poverty due to the high costs of custodial care. After a few meetings, we set up a LTCI plan that would pay the majority of their expenses for quite a while if either needed care.

Fast forward to a year ago. Donna hadn't been doing well. Her memory started going first. And then during a bout with the flu, things got worse. She could no longer drive, nor go shopping on her own, nor take a walk around the neighborhood. And all of her care was being provided by Fred.

Thankfully, they had the Long Term Care Insurance. It provided them with money to pay for Donna's care while she was at home. She was still active, but needed supervision in many activities. She went out with a *Senior's Club* two times a week and a Home Health Aid came in another 3 days a week to give Fred some time to run errands and go to the YMCA.

A few months ago, Donna's memory got substantially worse and Fred just couldn't take care of her at home any longer, even with the extra home care help she was getting. Donna now needed 24 hour care, more than Fred could handle at his age, so she entered a nursing home. Now, Donna can get the round-the-clock care she needs. Fred visits Donna every day and has much less stress knowing that Donna is in a safe environment and is being taken care of.

Again, Fred and Donna are thankful to have the Long Term Care Insurance to help pay for the Nursing Home stay. Because of the LTCI, Fred will be able to maintain control of his assets.

While their lives aren't the same as they were five years ago, both Fred and Donna have maintained their independence and dignity. Which is exactly what they wanted.

Contrast that situation with Chuck and Sue's situation. About 4 years ago – probably the same time that Fred and Donna were looking into LTCI, I reviewed Chuck and Sue's situation and we discussed the possibility as well.

"That's too expensive," replied Sue. "I want to make sure my kids get as much money as possible when I die. If we spend money on this, we won't have as much to give them."

Two years ago, we revisited the situation. Mostly due to Chuck's health. The first time we discussed this, he was ineligible to receive coverage because he had had a stroke shortly before. But after the 2 years without any medical problems, he was insurable again.

Unfortunately, Sue told me the same thing. "It's too expensive. Besides, if Chuck gets sick, I'll take care of him."

Well, Chuck **has** been sick. He is now completely uninsurable. And because of this, Sue has rethought her Long Term Care strategy.

"You know," she told me on the phone, "I think I might want to look at that Long Term Care Insurance again for just me. If something were to happen to me, I don't think Chuck would live through it."

You can already figure out what happened, right? Well, Sue has had *some minor medical issues* of her own. Nothing serious, but until they are under control, she is uninsurable as well. In addition, when she (hopefully) becomes insurable again, it will be at a significantly increased cost.

Thankfully, neither Chuck nor Sue needs any sort of care at this point. But I know their stress levels are elevated. They have **NO** safety net. If something happens, they need to cover it 100% out of their own pocket. And I know that scares them.

What Strategy Is Best?

Isn't that the true question? What strategy should I implement? What's best for me?

I can't tell you in a few pages what is best for you. To some extent, no one can. Again, we don't have a crystal ball to decide who needs what care in the future. All we can do is create a solid plan with the best information we have and know that we did our best.

There really are only 2 basic choices: LTCI and later-life gifting. LTCI is probably the hard choice. You are sticking your neck out on something you don't know for a fact will happen.

And gifting is easy. You either do it now and forget it, or tell yourself you'll gift it later on, when things look *bad*.

But I think back to what John F. Kennedy said in his in an address in September of 1962: *We choose to go to the moon in this decade and do the other things, not because they are easy, but because they are hard.* We do the hard thing because it is the right thing to do. Because it will save us untold heartache later on.

Gifting appears to be the best strategy **because** it is so easy – yet there are so many problems associated with it.

- You could lose all of your assets to a lawsuit, divorce, or accident.

- Gifting away IRA's and 401(k) plans require you to pay **all** the taxes on the plan before gifting the money away.

- You face the entire Medicaid system, with all of its bureaucracy, forms, and rule changes.

- You will not get to choose any of your Long Term Care plans. You can only go to the nursing home that the state has decided is best for you.

Honestly, it really **does** depend on your situation. Like we've been discussing all along, you need a plan. If that plan includes gifting because gifting is the right strategy for you – that's great. And if your plan includes purchasing LTCI – that's great too.

But we can't implement a plan we don't have, can we?

Estate Planning!

Where Small Mistakes Turn into BIG Dollars!

Probably one of the saddest things I have seen is a family who failed to plan for their ultimate demise and wasted thousands of dollars in needless expenses at death. It's a crime to see money that was supposed to go to the heirs end up in Uncle Sam's or some attorney's pocket.

One gentleman I dealt with flat-out refused to do any estate planning. He was never going to die. **Never!** Well, ultimately, he did die. And because he never did any planning, it cost his estate several hundred thousand dollars.

Another client passed away with a simple estate plan and a complicated estate. She left most of the settlement work to her attorney after her passing While the children were probably cheering for their six-figure settlement each, I'm sure Mom was rolling in her grave that it cost almost $50,000 to settle her fairly simple estate.

There are countless stories like this one. Of estates tied up for years, or invaded by unscrupulous attorneys. All because people don't want to face the fact that some day they will die.

Historical Perspective

Back when your grandparents passed away, life was much simpler. In the first place, the wealth that has flowed over to the middle class in the last 50 years hadn't happened yet. It's likely that your grandparents passed away with little or nothing to their names.

Housing prices weren't nearly as high as they are today – even when adjusted for 50 years of inflation. Few people invested in the stock market at all. The safe havens 50 years ago were the banks and the mattress. You didn't get much interest in either place. So there just wasn't a whole lot of estate to settle.

In addition, we didn't have IRA's and 401(k)'s and 403(b) plans. No one saved in a tax-deferred account for retirement – or if they did they used simple annuities which, like a pension, ended at death.

Finally, it seemed the courts were adequately staffed. It was not uncommon to have several people working in the probate court for a specific town or region. There was always help available in the form of numerous workers.

The Reality Today

Now it's different. People have more assets. *Much* more. They own houses worth several hundred thousand dollars. Bank accounts. CD's. Stocks. Bonds. Mutual Funds. Second and vacation homes. Time shares. People have lots of assets in lots of places.

And I know that for most of my clients, the IRA/401(k)/403(b) portion of their total estate is significant. Which means dealing with all sorts of distribution rules not only during lifetime, but after death as well – in addition to issues relating to the complicated IRD (Income in Respect to Decedent) rules.

Finally, the probate courts aren't staffed the way they used to be. Governments have reduced staffing over time by attrition. Long-time helpful court clerk Betty retires and they don't fill her position.

Sure, newer computerized systems help, but courts are more and more backlogged every day. The typical probate for an estate where I live takes well over a year now. Even for something as simple as a few checking accounts, a CD, and a house. A year – *minimum!*

Not only are the probate courts understaffed, but we have more people dying – if only due to the population increases we've seen over the past 40 years or so. A bigger population means more people are dying. So our courts are being attacked on both sides.

What is Probate?

Let me back up a bit and talk a little bit about probate. I find that many people, unless they've gone through an estate settlement, have some misconceptions about how probate works and who needs to use it.

First of all, anyone who owns things in their own name and has no will must go through probate. Virtually everyone I talk with understands this.

But someone with assets in their names and *has* a will also goes through probate as well. And that is something many people are unaware of.

Probate is for people with a will and without a will, provided they have sufficient assets.

"Wait a second," you're thinking. "If I have a will, what do I need probate for?

My thought EXACTLY! Why do you need probate if you know where everything is supposed to go? Why get bogged down in the government fees, processes and minutia?

Because the government says so.

Let's go back a minute to English Common Law – where most of our laws originated. Back several hundred years ago, probate was created so that no one person could unlawfully and unscrupulously seize all of decedent's (Decedent is a fancy word meaning the person who's died.

In this case it was almost always Dad, the lord of the estate) assets.

If you think back to a time with noblemen and inheritances and such, you can see that every heir **wanted** the courts to review a will and ensure everyone got their rightful fair share.

And that's just what a probate court does now.

Probate court reviews the will (if there is one) for accuracy, it determines if the heirs are legitimate, it appoints an *executor* or *administrator* to oversee the distribution of assets, and reviews the whole process to ensure that everyone got what they were supposed to get.

Along the way, you will receive delay after delay. You will have to notify the world that your mother, father, or other relative has passed away – and give everyone a right to review the will, contest it, and review what assets will pass to whom.

Oh, and the fees. I forgot the fees. Fees for the court, fees for your attorney. (You don't expect to do this yourself, do you?) Fees for the newspaper notices and other people waiting for their fair share of your estate.

Is There A Better Way?

Do we really need all of that? Is all of that necessary? If we know who should get what, and we trust that our heirs will do the right thing, do we need to go through that entire public, time consuming, costly process?

No! We thankfully don't.

We can avoid probate altogether. There are simple ways. There are complicated ways.

You see, probate is designed to play traffic cop for assets that don't know where they are going. For instance, if I own 1,000 shares of IBM in my name and I die, those shares don't know where to go and are required to go through probate.

But if you and I own 1,000 shares of IBM jointly and I die, you get to keep all 1,000 shares and never deal with probate.

Those shares *know* where they are going. As long as an asset knows where it's going, it doesn't *need* probate.

So your IRA with a beneficiary on it – doesn't need to go to probate. (As long as the beneficiary is alive when you die.)

Your life insurance will pass the same way.

Any property you own jointly will pass to the other party without any need for probate. Joint bank accounts, brokerage accounts and owning land in joint name are cheap ways to avoid probate.

Now the wheels are spinning, aren't they? As long as I put someone else's name on your assets, you can avoid probate, right?

As we discussed in the last chapter, putting someone's name on your asset, be it your home or your bank account, opens up the asset to any creditor of the other person.

So, for instance, you put your daughter's name on your bank account and also as joint-owner of your home. If your daughter gets divorced or sued or falls behind in her mortgage payments, both your money and your home are vulnerable to seizure by parties unknown.

Now, in all likelihood, you trust your children. I trust mine as well. But I don't know what circumstances might befall them in the future. I want to protect my assets for my own needs and for my children's future needs.

Another problem with just adding someone's name to an account is simultaneous death.

Let's say you own your home with your daughter. And on a celebratory vacation a giant cow falls on your car and kills both of you instantly. Now what happens to your home? If you guessed "it goes to probate" you have been paying attention.

A Better Solution: The Revocable Living Trust

There is one other solution to your probate problems. It's called a Living Trust. Also called a Revocable Living Trust, RLT, Loving Trust and a myriad of other names.

This trust is created by you or you and your spouse. It holds *all* of your assets for your lifetime. You become the *grantor* – the one who gives the money to the trust and the *trustee* – the one who manages the trust.

The trust contains a a stated list of beneficiaries similar to what you'd place in your will.

"I leave my utility stocks to my son Jeremy unless he predeceases me, then I would like my cousin Irving to have them." You can get *very* detailed with the beneficiary statement within a trust. Or you can keep it general such as "I leave all of my assets to my children, equally."

Because trust assets know where they are going, there is no need for them to pass through probate. Instead of an *executor* you have a *successor trustee*. And if the heirs don't trust the trustee (who is usually one of the beneficiaries in the first place), they can bring it **back** to the court and have the court watch the trustee for any misappropriation of funds.

What a trust allows you to do is settle the entire estate *under the radar.* You don't have the delays of probate. Your successor trustee only needs a copy of the trust and a death certificate to prove he or she is the trustee. There is no public

112

notification. All affairs are kept private. And because of the simplification, you can do most of the work yourself – saving thousands in probate and attorney's fees.

During your lifetime, your trust operates just as you would. It is revocable, which means you can change it or *revoke* it at any time. There is no special Tax ID number necessary. As far as Uncle Sam is concerned, your trust is a part of you.

The trust is effectively invisible until your death. You set up everything now to avoid probate, then manage it as you always have. When you die, the trust does exactly what you told it to do. It becomes (in most cases) that simple.

In addition, certain types of Living Trusts can help married couples avoid *estate taxes*. Estate taxes are nasty fees that you pay the government if you die with too many assets. State estate taxes begin at about one million dollars in Massachusetts and several million at the federal level.

Estate tax rates start at a nominal amount but quickly rise to up to 45%! Needless to say, anything that can be done to reduce this is significant. And the right Living Trust for a married couple can help reduce or eliminate those taxes.

Medical & Financial Directives

It has been several years, but we all remember the name Terry Schiavo. No matter which side of the battle you were on during her lifetime, you have to agree it was a complete disaster from beginning to end.

To refresh your memory, Terry suffered severe brain damage and entered a coma in 1990 after a heart attack at a very young age. She left no directives as to how to manage her money or her health in the event she was unable to make decisions on her own.

In the nightmare that followed, her husband Michael received legal *custody* of Terry and was given the right to make all of her medical decisions – including removing her feeding tube.

Terry's parents fought hard against this for several years. They stated that their daughter was adamant about maintaining a right to life while Michael maintained that, even without written documentation, Terry expressed a desire to not be kept alive via extraordinary means.

This entire battle unfolded in front of us on our television sets from 2002 through Terry's death in 2005. The overriding question in everyone's mind was, *"What did Terry want?"*

And we never knew.

Sadly, medical and financial directives are fairly easy to execute. Many attorneys will prepare them along with your other estate planning documents. All it takes is to sit down with a qualified estate planning attorney.

If It's So Easy – Why Don't Most People Have An Estate Plan?

Good question. Why don't most people have their wills drafted – and updated more than once a quarter-century? And have medical directives? And have trusts if needed?

I can think of two reasons. The first relates to attorneys. If you are an attorney, or love one more than life itself, you may want to skip a few paragraphs. I'm going to paint with a very broad brush. Not all attorneys fall under this category. But enough do so that it seems to us lay-people that every attorney works this way.

When we think of attorneys, we think of two things. Dollar signs and attitude. We know we are always on the clock when we are with them. We also know they have an disposition of "I'm right, you're wrong, accept it."

There are hundreds, if not thousands, of lawyer jokes relating to the above two issues. We all think it. Even if it isn't true.

So we delay. We see going to our attorney on par with going to the dentist. (Apologies to the dentists out there as well.) It's painful. It's expensive. And it's something that won't directly benefit me today. So why go through the pain? At least I leave the dentist looking better than I did when I came in!

The second reason people don't keep up with their estate planning relates to the psyche of the human animal. In order for us to survive, we avoid any thought of our very finite mortality. We just can't think about it and function normally.

Imagine this. You are walking around 20 years from now. Close your eyes and imagine it. Now imagine it's 40 years from now. Do it again. How about 60 years? 80? I know in every case, I do **not** see my wife and kids crying over my coffin. I imagine myself still doing the things I love.

That self-preservation image allows us to think, "Ahhh, this estate planning is silly. I'm going to live another 20, 30, 50, 100 years. Why should I bother with this?"

Yet every day, people have heart attacks. They get cancer. Errant cows land on their cars. I could be next. You could be next! We just don't know.

So we all need to have our plans in place **NOW**. Or else someone who shouldn't get any of your money at your death – like the government or one of those pesky lawyers – will get it. Or your wishes won't be carried out in the event of a coma or other incapacitating illness. As I said, we all need to have these plans in place and we need them now.

The Most Important Aspect Of Your Estate Plan!

There is one key ingredient to your estate plan that is absolutely essential – a qualified estate planning attorney that you can trust and talk to.

Estate Planning is a specialized field. Just like Asbestos Litigation and International Law. Yet it is taught – albeit briefly – to most law students so most attorneys believe they can create a good estate plan with sheer force of thought.

Unfortunately, sheer force of thought can get you in trouble in most complicated estate planning situations. I've seen clients with family businesses and multimillion dollar portfolios with just a will. "Oh, my attorney said he'd take care of me." I'm *sure* of that.

Or the attorney who put trust language within a will to "save the client money" yet ensured that the estate would be tied up in probate for decades. Or the client who had very few assets, yet was sold a large estate plan – including trust – which provided absolutely zero benefit to them.

In all these cases, attorneys who were "General Practitioners" were attempting to solve Estate Planning issues by sheer force of thought.

In addition, you need to find an attorney that is approachable and trustworthy. I'm sure you have met many who were the complete opposite of that. I have too.

How do you find this person? It isn't easy. You might luck out and a friend of yours or your financial advisor might know just the right person. Other than that, it's trial and error. But it must be done.

You might be in the majority of people who can get by with something simple that most attorneys should be able to do. But if you are in the growing minority that has some quirk that only an estate planning attorney will catch and fix, having the wrong person create your Estate Plan will only multiply your problems.

Where To Go From Here?

If you are anything like the people I meet with every day, your head is probably spinning with all of these terms and concepts. Thoughts of how the estate tax laws interact with the probate process and income tax laws. This is on top of issues relating to the Long Term Care problems we addressed in the last chapter.

For example, let's say you want to give your son or daughter $50,000 to help them buy a house. How many different rules does this affect? Potentially, all four:

1. There is a gift limit of $14,000 per person (2016), per year. This does not necessarily mean that if you gift more, then you will pay taxes. But at the very least, you will be required to fill out a Form 709 with the IRS. And if you've made significant gifts in the past, this *might* trigger a gift/estate tax.

2. A gift of that size will disqualify you from any sort of Medicaid assistance for approximately 5 months. (And that disqualification stays with you for the next 5 years!)

3. If you sell property, stocks, or some asset to raise the necessary funds, you will likely owe income taxes. If you gift the asset outright (as in deeding land, or gifting stock certificates), your son or daughter is responsible for the same income taxes if and when they sell the asset.

4. A gift of a specific asset may also affect your estate plan. Depending on how you structured your will and/or trust, the estate may be ultimately unbalanced because of this gift.

And that's just with a relatively "small" gift of $50,000. Think about how complicated things might get when you start working with your entire estate.

Each and every decision you make affects four different areas: Estate/Gift taxes, Estate Settlement, Income Taxes, and Long Term Care. The rules are complicated and sometimes get blurred together. This is a lot of information to process at once.

This is one area I rarely recommend people tackle themselves. If you've ever thought about getting some sort of professional help regarding your finances, this is where to start. Getting an expert to help wade through all of these rules is crucial to a successful plan that will allow you to protect your assets from Estate Taxes, Long Term Care and Probate.

Listening to the Wrong People!

Your Biggest Financial Mistake!

Finances are one of those funny categories. You can ask 50 people and everyone has an opinion and rarely do they have anything to back it up.

Way back in Chapter 2, we talked about not having a plan. Just as bad – or perhaps worse - is having a plan but basing it on false or misleading information because you listened to the wrong people.

When planning for your retirement, the mistake you make may not be noticeable until you are 70 years old or older. Then what do you do? You can't go back to work as easily as you did when you were 35.

Friends, Family & Coworkers

The first group of people we need to filter out are the folks around you. Everyone is willing to share an opinion. And every opinion is offered as Gospel fact. I can't tell you how many times I've had to explain that the *fact* given to them by a coworker was blatantly wrong. And in many of those situations, relying on that fact would have caused severe financial harm to my client.

Even with innocuous facts, we want to get the story right. A few years ago, I was talking with an employee of a large regional firm about the firm's company stock. He explained in minute detail the reasoning behind their poor performance.

"The CEO's biggest fear right now is that the stock goes up and all the employees exercise their stock options. They can't afford to do that so they are keeping the price down."

I was speechless. The CEO, option program and employees' financial decisions have little, if any effect on the day-to-day movements of the stock. Yet he was convinced of this. Had he relied on this erroneous factoid to plan his retirement, he could be in serious trouble.

I won't go into detail of how many times I've been told things about the company 401(k) plan or tax breaks or mortgages which were completely wrong. The bottom line is this: If you had a sharp pain in your chest, would you rather see a doctor or the guy in the next office? The same should be true about your finances as well.

The Financial Press

CNN, MSNBC, Fox News, CNBC. I hate every single one of these channels. Especially during the daytime.

There are 24 hours in the day. Out of each hour, there are approximately 40 minutes of "air" to fill after taking out commercials, introductions, and closing credits. So cable news stations have to fill 40 minutes in every hour, 24 hours a day.

That's 960 minutes per day, every day. They have to fill that time with *news*. With whatever *news* they can find. Therefore, anyone with a pulse becomes an expert on the economy, oil, the market, or whatever. It's constant opinions. And the more controversial the opinion, the better the ratings.

People ask which channel I watch. None of them! I go out of my way not to watch cable news. . . . or even broadcast news. Outside of a doctor's office or a airport, I never see a news channel on TV.

In fact, a few years ago, I was watching cable news at a friend's house. As one program was finishing up, someone recommended a particular investment as a strong buy. After the commercial break, another *expert* came on and listed that **same investment** as a strong sell.

Now we all chuckle at that. And it's not surprising. But where we get into trouble is when **we accept these opinions as fact!**

I don't want to pick on the cable news industry. This is just as true for financial talk radio and the print media. I still enjoy reading the covers of the financial magazines (*Money, Smart Money, Forbes, etc.,*) in the store. Every month lists the best mutual funds to own today. Or the five best funds for the next century. Or the 17 top funds. Everything is best or top or greatest or whatever.

In reality, they are almost **always** looking at last year's performance. **SO WHAT?!** I don't care what XYZ fund did last year. It doesn't help me at all picking funds that will do well **THIS** year, will it?

Keep this in mind: Whether it's *Money Magazine* or CNBC or The Dave Ramsey Radio Show, all of them are there for one ultimate reason – to sell commercial time. Helping you is the hook to keep you interested. The advice they offer is generic and may or may not apply to your situation. Following them because it sounds like a good idea – without knowing the effects that strategy will have on *your* situation – is asking for problems in the future.

Trusting Yourself

This is the hardest person to ignore – yourself. I won't lie to you. Retirement is not rocket science. Outside some complicated tax code, probate rules, and Long Term Care regulations, it really isn't *that* hard. But it takes a lot of careful, objective, unemotional planning. Something that is difficult when dealing with your own money.

REAL LIFE STORY: You Can't Think Your Way Out Of Some Situations!

A very good client of mine called me up once. He was 57, recently retired, and was in need of some money. Fast!

Fred (not his real name) is an engineer. Now I love engineers. They deal with facts. But sometimes one fact can cloud the situation and cause other, more pertinent facts, to disappear.

What am I talking about? Well, let me tell you this brief story.

Fred called me up and said he needed $20,000. Even though our plan was to take that money from a small account he held onto elsewhere, he insisted that we take it from his IRA.

"Fred," I explained. "If we do this, we'll need to continue distributions until age 62 – with no deviation. (Remember the rules pertaining to distributions prior to age 59½.) If you take it from that other account, you can have whatever you need whenever you need it for the next two years. Once you hit 59½, we can do the same with your IRA."

"But my other account is performing better in the last six months! I'd rather take it from my IRA."

(Remember what we talked about regarding time horizon in Chapter 5?)

"I agree. Because your IRA is invested differently, it has a different return. But this isn't an investment decision; it's a tax decision."

"I understand that," Fred replied. "But the facts are facts – the other account is doing better. I shouldn't be selling that now."

Fred had all the information. He had the tax regulations. He had the allocations of both investments. He had the rate of return information correct to the 2nd decimal place. What he didn't have was a clear understanding of his entire situation

He was technically correct. And by making his technically correct decision, he was going to paint himself into a financial corner. He had no understanding of his personal situation because he was too close to see it.

You know the old saying, "You can't see the forest for the trees," right? That was Fred. He was so focused on one single issue that he couldn't pick his head up. Why?

Emotions!

I often think that the biggest reason I can make good financial decisions for my clients is because it isn't my money. I can view their situation with complete objectivity.

Your Uncle Frank won't be mad at me if I recommend you not lend him the $10,000 because he's not *my* Uncle Frank. I can evaluate the financial ramifications of the condo in Ft. Myers because *I* haven't fallen in love with the beach at that resort. And I can make a tax decision of which account you should take money from in any given year because *I* haven't fallen in love with the performance of one particular account.

All of those extraneous items that cloud our judgment are missing for me. It's not *my* money!

Because of this, it's incredibly difficult for you to do this 100% on your own. At the very least, you need someone to bounce ideas off of. And I don't mean a spouse, friend, or relative. They can get caught up in your emotions just as easily. Or give you bad advice out of ignorance as we saw a few pages ago.

You need someone unbiased. Someone who will look at your situation objectively and can help you wade through the decisions.

But who can you trust? Isn't that the real problem: Finding someone you can trust to help you with your financial decisions?

Bad Advisors

Unfortunately, it isn't easy to find a financial advisor who has your best interest at heart. Almost the entire industry is designed around selling you something instead of helping you.

In addition, there are more inexperienced advisors who have no idea about personal finance. In many cases, you know more than the person across the kitchen table from you.

The existing business model in financial services isn't that much different from the auto industry. I sometimes say that your average financial advisor is just a used car salesman in a better suit.

Most advisors in the industry rely on commissions to earn a living. Now let me say that commissions by themselves are not bad. Nor are people who earn commissions automatically bad people. In fact, there are some financial products that are next to impossible to purchase without paying a commission.

But what the commission system does is reward an advisor for bringing in a new client. There is little to no incentive to care for an existing clients.

The typical commission on an investment sale is around 5%. For every $100,000 you invest, the broker and brokerage firm earn about $5,000. That is paid within a month of you investing your money.

A year later, the broker and firm might receive another $250. That's it.

Where should that broker invest his time a year or two from now? On you and your $100,000 or a new person who they can get to invest a new $100,000?

The industry has rigged the system so that a broker's main focus is not on servicing his or her clients, but on selling more and more stuff to new people.

Sure, the big brokerage firms and insurance companies air all those commercials and slogans during golf tournaments and the Super Bowl. They create marketing campaigns to show how committed they are to servicing existing clients. But when the rubber meets the road, the brokers get paid the most to find new clients, not service old ones. Thus all the advertising.

Again, I'm not saying that there are no good advisors. Just that the industry as a whole stacks the deck against your finding someone who actually cares about you.

Is There A Solution?

Well we know we can't listen to our friends and the financial press. They are offering generic – and many times wrong – advice. And we can't trust ourselves to make decisions completely by ourselves. And the financial industry is set up so that a broker's focus is on himself, not on us. Is there any way to get the advice we need?

Thankfully, the answer is **YES!**

In the last 40 years, some advisors have subscribed to a different business model – one I've believed in since I started in this business in 1991. It is called fee-based financial planning.

The first commitment of this model is to focus on the planning first. Remember we talked about that in Chapter 2. Having a plan and implementing it is a key first step in a successful retirement.

The second commitment is to scrap the upside-down commission structure that pervades the brokerage industry. Instead of commissions, we get paid fees.

What's the difference?

Remember above when I said that a typical broker will receive about 5% up front to invest your assets and little else afterwards? Well in a fee arrangement, we turn that system right-side-up.

Typically, my clients pay a yearly fee of between 0.50% and 1.00% of their total portfolio under management. A huge drop from 5-6% right?

Over time, I will make far more money than a commission broker. Why? Because I get that fee each and every year. And if I don't do my job to your satisfaction, **you can fire me and I receive no more fees!**

So where is my emphasis? On finding new clients or taking care of my existing clients?

Do you see how this allows an advisor to focus on planning first? Their concern is for their clients' entire well-being. My ultimate goal as a fee-based planner is to be a client's advisor for life. And taking care of those clients for life means focusing on all areas of their financial decisions.

THIS is how money management should be. And it's also the reason the big brokerage firms and insurance companies will never be able to follow this business model – they would literally starve attempting to implement it. They can't get away from the overly-profitable model of high up-front commissions and high client turnover.

What's Your Next Step?

Believe it or not, it's probably your **first** step.

If you agree that there are too many things to know. That there are too many decisions to make. That this is too important to try and go it alone – you need to find an advisor.

If you happen to live in the Eastern Massachusetts/Rhode Island area – you might even consider contacting me personally. I would welcome that openly. In the back of this book is a short biography of me and my company. It discusses what we do and how we do it. If that makes sense to you and seems to fit with what you are looking for, I encourage you to contact me.

I offer every person who receives a copy of this book (whether you bought it at a store or borrowed it from a friend) the opportunity to meet with me one-on-one to discuss your situation. A *Financial Physical* if you will. Basically, it's a no cost, 30-minute meeting to discuss any issues you might have. And if you haven't picked up on my style yet, this is as high-sales as it gets.

I want to work with people who want to work with me. Why would anyone willingly try to work with someone whom they didn't like? Remember, I don't want to hit you over the head until you buy something. I want you to be a client for life.

What will we discuss in our meeting?

1. I will try to answer any questions you may have.
2. I will let you know about any financial problems that I might see in your situation.
3. We will decide if there is a need for us to work together for the future.

If that makes sense to you, I encourage you to contact my office and set up an appointment. I would love to get a chance to talk with you more about your personal situation.

And if our personalities fit well together and there is a need for us to work together, that's great. If not, that's OK too.

Finding an advisor you can trust is difficult. I understand that. So I offer this to you to help you get to know me better.

Last Thoughts

Well, that's it. I hope that you have gleaned some information about your situation and how to view it differently. Retirement is not easy. We only get one chance at doing it successfully. I wish you good luck in your financial future.

Biography

Dennis J. O'Keefe, CFP® is owner of ***Successful Money Strategies, Inc.*** in Fall River, MA. He has been advising individuals on their personal financial goals since 1991.

The majority of Dennis' clients are retirees and soon-to-be-retirees between the ages of 50 and 70. Many are retirees of Verizon/Bell Atlantic/NYNEX/AT&T. He regularly advises employees and retirees of the other local utilities on a frequent basis as well.

Retirement is a difficult process. And we only get one chance at it. That is why Dennis has made it his specialty. Some advisors specialize in college planning. Or young families. Or debt management. Dennis specializes in probably the most stressful area of planning due to the many regulations and limited time and resources afforded to his clients.

Dennis graduated from Bentley College and has attained his Certified Financial Planner® designation. He is a committed husband and father who lives in Southeastern Massachusetts with his wife and four children.

You can contact Dennis via email at *dennis@successfulmoney.com*

[i] http://www.ssa.gov/pressoffice/basicfact.htm
[ii] http://www.bls.gov/opub/ted/2001/May/wk3/art03.htm
[iii] $15,720. 2015 Social Security Administration.
[iv] USInflationCalculator.com
[v] Ibbotson SBBI 2015
[vi] Source: longtermcare.gov, 2012
[vii] Source: US Dept of Heath & Human Services © 2005

Made in the USA
Middletown, DE
18 November 2023

42875452R00077